JOURNEY TO GENNESARET

NAVIGATING STORMS ON THE JOURNEY TO SPIRITUAL GROWTH

KALE HORVATH

ISBN: 978-1-7117364-5-7

All Scripture quotations are from the Authorized King James Version of the Bible.

Edited by Tricia Van Sickle

Cover Photo by Ian Espinosa on Unsplash.com

DEDICATION

To my wife, Brooke. You are my best friend, and my biggest fan. Thank you for always believing in me.

CONTENTS

ACKNOWLEDGMENTS

Thank you to my Lord Jesus Christ, who continues to use me despite myself. For He is good and His mercy endures forever. Thank you to my church family, First Baptist Church of New Philadelphia, Ohio, for raising me, teaching me, training me, and guiding me to where I am today. Thank you to Tricia for editing this book and teaching me more about grammar, voice, and tone—you're smarter than all of us, and it's really not fair at all.

Journey to Gennesaret

PREFACE

Preaching is simply pleading with men to heed God's word.

Preaching the Bible is not difficult, though rightly dividing it so that you don't preach it incorrectly is. It takes time, work, prayer, honesty, and devotion to compare scripture with scripture and properly extract God's truth from the text, rather than inserting your own presupposition or bias. Then, you must work to prepare it for presentation, putting "handles" on the message so that the hearer can apply it to their lives. That is the job of the preacher. To take God's word, as God has authoritatively preserved it, and boldly proclaim it as the prophets of old–Thus saith the Lord! Begging men and women–pleading with them–to heed the truth of the message.

To rightly divide the Scripture, one must understand that there are three applications for each verse found within its pages, be it

Old or New Testament. The first and foremost application of scripture is historical. The Bible is predominantly a history book. It is not a book of fables, myths, or allegory–its contents are historical fact. All the stories contained within those pages of Holy Writ are actual happenings of men and women who lived lives, breathed air, and spoke words. The battles that take place are real battles that happened in real locations around the globe, on literal pieces of land where the blades of grass and grains of sand collected the drops of blood spilt. If you deny the historical authenticity and veracity of the Bible, then you are forgoing any power it may have in your life before even getting started.

God, who "cannot lie" (Titus 1:2), promised to preserve every "jot and tittle" of the Bible until "heaven and earth pass" (Matthew 5:18). If there is even *one* error or contradiction in this book, then God ceases to be God–on the authority of His own words! So, to allegorize the creation week, or question the historical veracity of Methuselah's age is simply to open the Book with the presupposition that God is not God, or, that God is not powerful enough to preserve His very words for us today. Although, one may capitulate that He was powerful enough to inspire them originally, when push comes to shove. If either option is the conviction of the reader, it begs the question, "Why bother?" Why bother going to a Book that is centuries old for help, guidance, and answers to life's deepest questions if you won't trust that it is what it claims to be?

Second, the Bible is a book of doctrine, or teaching. Each event recorded in the Scripture has historical truth, but it also has doctrinal application to somebody somewhere. That is what separates the Bible from every other book ever written. The doctrinal application is also referred to as the prophetic application, because many times the doctrinal teaching is a prophesy pointing to events yet future.

Many prophesies found in the Old Testament have already been fulfilled, such as the many prophetic references pointing to the birth and life of Jesus Christ. Some are still awaiting fulfillment. But, many of those prophetic passages referred, historically, to someone else, all the while pointing to Someone yet future. That is the power of the Scripture. Some passages even point backwards, such as Isaiah 14 and Ezekiel 28, which tell us about the fall of Lucifer that happened in dateless past. Yet, the prophets writing those were real men who lived and wrote at some point in history. See how those two applications exist simultaneously?

This is the job of the preacher; to study the Word "line upon line, precept on precept, here a little, there a little" (Isaiah 28:10), so as to expose the truth of God's Word without contradicting it. That is how heresy is born—when someone "privately interprets" (2 Peter 1:20) the Scripture without making sure that it jives with the rest of the Bible. Context is key to understand anything that anyone has ever said, and so much more so when trying to understand what the Creator of the Universe is trying to say to you today. You owe it to yourself, and to God, to understand what He said, in the context of how He said it, and to whom He said it.

The third application of scripture is the devotional application, also known as the inspirational or personal application. This is the heart and soul of preaching that allows men's hearts to be convicted and encouraged by the Word of God. It is the means by which the historical understanding and doctrinal teaching are placed in the hands of the hearers that they may actually apply it to their lives today. A sermon comprised of only historical and doctrinal application is merely a lesson for the furtherance of knowledge for intellect's sake—which is great, actually, in the context of the classroom. Teaching affects the mind, but preaching is to affect the heart. Preaching should convict a man to align his life with what the Bible says with such power and authority that the change is permanent, and not the inspirational cat poster of a fleeting moment. Anyone can articulate an inspirational sentiment, but only a preacher with the infallible words of God in His hands can change the lives of someone forever, for there is power in his message.

> *2 Timothy 4:2 Preach the word; be instant in season, out of season; reprove, rebuke, exhort with all longsuffering and doctrine.*

Unfortunately, in these last days, many pastors don't understand, or don't care to put the work in to understand, all three of these applications: historical, doctrinal, and devotional. Balancing these three and comparing scripture with scripture is the only way to understand God's Word without contradicting it or creating a private interpretation. While there is power in the devotional side of scripture, many *only* preach that application.

Their sermon is comprised only of stories from their personal life, sprinkled with some verses, and concluded by some inspirational, spiritual-sounding tidbit offered in compact form perfect for tweeting or quoting on a coffee mug. It is hard to find a preacher today (although they do exist, if you'll only search!) who will give you the good with the bad, the rebuke with the exhortation, the inspiration with the doctrine and history. Preaching is not self-elevating, social networking, or private marketing. Preaching is pleading with men to heed God's Word.

So, why do I say all that as an introduction to this book? I say this because I am a preacher by trade, not an author. I am a pastor, not a promoter. I am not writing this book as a means of future retirement planning. I have written this book to expose the truth of God's Word to you, so that it may change your life—*if* you'll allow it.

This book is a devotional commentary on a short passage in Matthew chapter 14. I say that because it is not a doctrinal study of the passage. Many more pages could be written exploring the doctrinal implications of the text, including but not limited to the very deity of Christ as He walks on the water and commands His power over nature by calming the sea. This book is a look at a story that clearly happened in history to real men that the Scripture records. Its purpose is to demonstrate how to apply the truths found in the passage to your own life.

This passage has very special meaning to me, as God used it mightily during a very difficult time in my life. As I "preach" to you from this text and include a few anecdotes from my own personal story, I hope that you will be encouraged and that your faith will be made stronger. I hope that your faith in Christ will gain a renewed sense of power that might have been lost during whatever catastrophic event you've experienced.

But, most of all, I hope that this book will give you faith in the words of God. The Bible is the *only* book in all of human history that can change lives. The book that you are reading right now is nothing. The only reason I wrote it down is because I wanted to personally remember the details of my story and what God has taught me, and because it is a bit too long to be a sermon delivered on a Sunday morning. It is the Word of God, and nothing else, that can change you. As such, this book contains many references from the Bible. Please do not skip over them. Read them. Meditate on the Scriptures. Memorize them. Love them. Apply them. Without the Scripture, the pages of this book would be blank, as I would have no message. It is the words of God Himself that have the power to break chains and calm seas. The words of men have no power of themselves. But, if those words are conveying the truths of God's words, they can surely change lives.

1 Corinthians 1:21 For after that in the wisdom of God the world by wisdom knew not God, it pleased God by the foolishness of preaching to save them that believe.

Romans 10:17 So then faith cometh by hearing, and hearing by the word of God.

So, dear reader, I hope the following pages will convey to you the truth of God's word, coupled with my personal experience of applying them to my own life. I hope that your takeaway from this book will be encouragement, as well as faith to keep pursuing God through the storm that you are currently experiencing, or that you will one day inevitably experience. Though, none of these things will matter if you don't have a healthy view of who God is and what His Bible is. I beg of you, dear reader, to heed the words of God.

Journey to Gennesaret

INTRODUCTION

"Why is this happening to me? "

This is just one of the millions of questions that were racing through my mind. I didn't understand. Wasn't I doing things right? Wasn't I doing exactly what He told me to do? I mean, maybe I had misheard His plan. Maybe I wasn't doing the right things. I was beginning to think that I had misunderstood where exactly He had told me to go. I was beginning to doubt. I was frustrated. I was angry. I was frightened. I was... sinking.

Many times, people go through trials in life that seem unnecessary or, at the very least, inconvenient. Depending on what culture you live in, you may deem an event a "trial" that doesn't seem cataclysmic to someone of a different background. The thing about tribulation is that it is completely subjective to the environment in which you live. I'm about to communicate something that I went through in my life and continue to live with every day. I'm not trying to say that it is the worst thing that could ever happen to someone, nor am I saying that my tribulation is equal to that of a starving child in a third world country. The intent of my writing this book is just to tell my story and share with you what God is teaching me through it.

What I've learned is that Christ wants to draw His sons and daughters closer to Him through the storms of life. But drawing is different than pulling. God never pulls. He draws. Pulling requires no effort on the part of the "pull-ee"; it actually may act against their will. Drawing is merely leading. And anyone being drawn always has the choice to not follow the leader.

> *Matthew 14:22-24*
> *22 And straightway Jesus constrained his disciples to get into a ship, and to go before him unto the other side, while he sent the multitudes away.*
> *23 And when he had sent the multitudes away, he went up into a mountain apart to pray: and when the evening was come, he was there alone.*
> *24 But the ship was now in the midst of the sea, tossed with waves: for the wind was contrary.*

This familiar story in Matthew 14 begins with Jesus telling His disciples to get into a ship and cross the sea of Galilee. It appears that Jesus is just going to meet them on the other side, because he sends them "before him" (vs 22) while he sent the multitudes of people away. Like good disciples, the twelve obey their Rabbi and make for the sea. While they are doing this, Jesus then travels up to a mountain to pray and does so until the evening. Now the story begins to unfold. The disciples are alone—well, by themselves. Jesus is not currently with them on the ship. It's at this time that a storm blows in and starts a series of events that I'm sure the disciples would never forget, especially Peter.

What exactly is a storm? Well, a weather storm is usually defined as a violent disturbance in the atmosphere. Typically, a storm has mass amounts of precipitation, cumulating with wind, thunder, and lightning. This mixture creates an unfavorable environment for humans and animals alike to be outside. Frequently, both men and creatures flee for shelter from the elements. Without some sort of shelter, the forces of a storm can cause injury or even death in severe circumstances. Storms will halt all plans of transportation, whether local or commercial. If rain falls hard enough, visibility is jeopardized and creates havoc for motorists. Depending on the severity of a storm, flights can be delayed or even cancelled for safety precautions. If occurring on a body of water, large waves and even hurricanes form. These can cause boats to be ported or capsized in severe conditions. The worse a storm becomes, the less likely it is that you or anyone else is going anywhere. And this is precisely where we find the disciples in Matthew chapter 14.

Isn't that how storms seem to start in your life? Jesus tells you to do something, so you begin to do it. Sometimes you aren't completely sure why He has given you the instructions He has, but you eventually obey like a good little disciple. Then, on the journey to this divine destination you assume Christ needs you to reach as soon as humanly possible, a storm hits.

So, let's get practical. We often equate trials and tribulations in our lives to storms. It's not uncommon to liken unfavorable circumstances to a storm. So, I think it's fair to draw some parallels between an atmospheric disturbance and the tribulations we may face in our own lives. A storm is any event that "upsets the waters" of our life. Or, to use a different analogy, a storm is an event that disturbs our "transportation" from where we are, to where we are headed. Storms will often hinder you from traveling to your destination, whether it be from God or your flesh. Storms prevent movement and therefore cause immobility and stagnancy. The storm in Matthew 14 caused the ship they were sailing to stop moving because the "wind was contrary", i.e., the wind was blowing in the opposite direction of where they were headed. In the parallel passage in Mark chapter 6, God says that the disciples were "toiling in rowing", which means that the sails were no longer of use to them. Because the winds of the storm were so great and blowing in the wrong direction, the crew actually abandoned the sails and started rowing. But this word "toiling" means simply that they weren't getting anywhere. They were working extremely hard and gaining almost no ground. And that is what storms do. The swirling winds of circumstance and travail cause us to cease forward momentum. *The worst thing that a storm can do is cause us to be stationary.*

A while ago I found myself in a similar situation. I felt God had given me pretty clear instruction on what to do and where to go. I was loading up the ship and shoving off—when all of a sudden my left tackle tripped, and I was blindsided by a 285 lb. pass rusher of a storm that knocked me flat on my derriere. I had no idea what had hit me, and I found myself "toiling in rowing" just to stay afloat.

Have you ever felt like this? Have you ever ditched the sails and started paddling just trying to stay alive? Well, you're not alone. I hope that as my story unfolds over the next few pages I can effectively communicate one thing to you: God's Word has all the answers. You can always find the answers to life's problems and predicaments in the pure and inerrant words of God. If you believe that and trust God to reveal to you what your next step is, He will. He did for me, and Matthew 14 is precisely the passage God illuminated to me in the darkness of my storm. This is my journey to Gennesaret.

CHAPTER 1

BEFORE THE DISCIPLES' STORM

Before we look at the storm the disciples are stuck in, we need to back up a bit and set the stage for the story. Every good story has a beginning, and this one is no different. In fact, what transpires directly before this story has everything to do with why the disciples are stuck in the storm. If we can understand why storms happen, perhaps we will have a better perspective of our circumstances during the storm, as the rain falls and the waves crash around us.

The story of the disciples caught in the storm begins in Matthew chapter 14, verse 22. But, the eight verses that precede the story set the stage for us. Matthew 14:14-21 tells the story of "The Feeding of the Five Thousand."

Matthew 14:14-21

14 And Jesus went forth, and saw a great multitude, and was moved with compassion toward them, and he healed their sick.

15 And when it was evening, his disciples came to him, saying, This is a desert place, and the time is now past; send the multitude away, that they may go into the villages, and buy themselves victuals.

16 But Jesus said unto them, They need not depart; give ye them to eat.

17 And they say unto him, We have here but five loaves, and two fishes.

18 He said, Bring them hither to me.

19 And he commanded the multitude to sit down on the grass, and took the five loaves, and the two fishes, and looking up to heaven, he blessed, and brake, and gave the loaves to his disciples, and the disciples to the multitude.

20 And they did all eat, and were filled: and they took up of the fragments that remained twelve baskets full.

21 And they that had eaten were about five thousand men, beside women and children.

To properly parse this passage and extract all the amazing historical and doctrinal implications would fill another book. So, a light study will have to suffice. First of all, verse 21 says that all who had eaten "were about five thousand *men*, beside women and children." This figure only includes the men who were there. If we were to guess that there were just as many women present, give or take, that puts the figure closer to ten thousand people, and that's not even factoring in children! We know that children were present, because John 6:9 tells us that the fish and bread used for the miracle were provided by a "lad". So, it is safe to say that Jesus turned five pieces of bread and two fish into enough food to feed over ten thousand people. That's amazing!

Think about how many people that is for a second: ten thousand. How many people are in your church on a given Sunday morning? 50? 100? 500? 1,000? Whatever that number is, imagine the size of that crowd. Then, think about how much larger a crowd of 10,000 would look like. If your church auditorium usually has 100 people in it on a Sunday, multiply that by 100, and you have a decent idea of how many people Jesus and the disciples fed.

So, this miracle is pretty special. Not only does Jesus feed this incredibly large crowd with a boy's lunch and have twelve baskets left over…but this is the only miracle, besides the resurrection of Christ, that is mentioned in all four gospels. That's a big deal. Jesus performed many miracles during His earthly ministry. From turning water to wine, to healing the sick, to raising the dead, Jesus did many things. But aside from His own resurrection from the dead, the only other miracle that is mentioned in all four gospel accounts is this feeding of the five (more like ten!) thousand. What does this mean? Well, you can read many things into it, but at the very least it means that this miracle affected a lot of people. Matthew, Mark, Luke, and John were four different men, who had four different personalities and perspectives. But this miracle left such an impact, they all thought that it was necessary to record it in their gospel account.

IMAGINE IF…

So practically, think about the impact this would have made on the twelve disciples. I feel like sometimes we strip the disciples of their humanity and personalities and subject them to "cartoon-ification"; or, we at least think of them as some distant historical figure, like George Washington or Thomas Edison. Obviously, these people existed, but we have never met them. Our grandparents never met them. So, although they were real, we only know them by their notable accomplishments, shortcomings, and what is documented about their lives. But, remember, the twelve disciples were real people, with real emotions and personalities. How did this event impact their lives?

For that matter, how did following Jesus at all impact their lives? Can you imagine what it would be like to give up your career at the drop of a hat, because some guy walked by and said, "Follow Me"? Don't divorce the story from history. This really happened to real people. Can you imagine watching this man teach like no one has ever taught from scripture before? Can you imagine watching him heal a leper, or a blind man, and watch that person's delight and amazement as their physical infirmity was lifted because of the Man you are following? Can you imagine growing so close to this Man for over three years, truly believing that He was who He said He was, Christ the Messiah, then watching Him die on a cross, wondering if you spent the last three years of your life following a phony? Can you imagine the amazing joy of seeing your once dead Rabbi, risen again, scars and all, confirming everything He had taught you, and reaffirming your faith?

Now that you are imagining things, imagine going out on the town (well, a desert, actually) with Jesus, and this enormous group of people listening to Him speak and watching Him heal. This isn't your first rodeo. At this point, you've seen Jesus do miracles before, so after a long day of helping Jesus and watching Him heal sick people, you speak up with the other disciples and say, "Jesus, we're in a desert. It's evening. We're tired. These guys are tired. They're probably hungry too. Send them away so that they can go into the villages and get something to eat." (Matthew 14:15 paraphrased by me)

Then, imagine Jesus saying, "They don't need to go anywhere. You guys give them some food." Can you imagine your reaction? Would it be something like, "Are you serious? What makes you think I can do something like that?" Remember how big this crowd is? It would seem pretty unrealistic that anyone had enough food for ten thousand people in their backpack.

So, you look around, and see some child open his lunch pail and pull out five pieces of bread and two fish. The child graciously offers to give them to you to help out, but you sarcastically tell Jesus, "See, look, all we have are five loaves and two fish. That's not quite enough to help these people." But Jesus knows what He's doing. And more often than not, He's trying to teach us something in the process. He says, "Bring them hither to me."

Now, imagine the disciples' reaction as they pass out enough food to feed all the people, and then some! How did Jesus do it? I don't really know. Did He give some to each disciple in a basket and as they went around to pass out food, every time they reached in the basket there was yet another piece of fish and bread? Could be. The Bible doesn't specify how it happened. But what we do know is that "they did all eat, *and* were filled; and they took up of the fragments that remained twelve baskets full." (Matthew 14:20)

This would have been extraordinary! They would have never seen anything like this. I imagine that even though it was later in the day at this point, the disciples would have been rejuvenated. I would have been! Think about it, if you were one of the twelve disciples you would have just seen Jesus perform an amazing miracle, right in front of you. And, you got to help! Sure, you personally didn't multiply the bread, but you helped pass it out. You were directly involved in serving people as Jesus got the glory. How awesome is that?

STRAIGHTWAY...

Now, we come to our story. Matthew 14:22 says, "And *straightway* Jesus constrained his disciples to get into a ship, and to go before him unto the other side, while he sent the multitudes away." Straightway just means immediately, or without delay. So, immediately after the feeding of the five thousand, Jesus constrained (compelled or urged) his disciples to get on a boat, cross the sea of Galilee, and go to Gennesaret. They were to go "before" him, because He would stay and send the multitudes away, but He would join them on the other side.

Now that you understand the setting, think about how the disciples were feeling when Jesus asked them to do this. I think they would have been excited. They had just witnessed the greatest miracle of Jesus' ministry up to that point, and they had a hand in it! They saw the power of God working right before their eyes. Surely, they would have been chomping at the bit to move on to whatever miracle Jesus had planned next.

Maybe they boarded the ship with pure elation, like a weary but encouraged team of church members boarding a plane home from a fruitful mission trip. Maybe they walked toward the ship with a little extra pep in their step, like a young lady who just led her best friend to the Lord after praying for her for years. Maybe they recounted the miracle, thought by thought, memory by memory, as they moved forward, like a pastor on his way back to his cabin after a night of preaching at summer camp, which led to three teenagers accepting Christ as their Savior.

How did they feel? I don't know exactly, but I do know how it feels to watch God work miraculously, right before my very eyes. I know what it feels like to lead a friend to the Lord. I know what it feels like to baptize a new believer. I know what it's like to come home from a summer camp for orphans in Hungary where 28 children accepted Christ as their Savior. I know what it's like to be on the spiritual mountain top—it's amazing! God feels so real to you. Of course, God is real, you know that. But *now* your faith is stronger than it has ever been before. You may not have seen Jesus transfigured on the mountain top, but you came as close as you've ever been. You saw Jesus work, and you are on a whole new level of spiritual joy!

Isn't it interesting that it is *immediately* after the spiritual mountain top, that these disciples get caught in a debilitating storm?

> *Matthew 14:22-24*
> *22 And straightway Jesus constrained his disciples to get into a ship, and to go before him unto the other side, while he sent the multitudes away.*
> *23 And when he had sent the multitudes away, he went up into a mountain apart to pray: and when the evening was come, he was there alone.*
> *24 But the ship was now in the midst of the sea, tossed with waves: for the wind was contrary.*

Has this ever happened to you? Have you ever witnessed the obvious outpouring of God in your life, only to almost immediately be met with a monstrous storm? That is exactly what the disciples are experiencing. Have you ever found yourself in the middle of a storm, toiling in rowing, asking yourself, how did this happen? It wasn't but a couple of weeks ago that you were standing on a spiritual pinnacle, gazing out across creation, beholding how wonderful God is, and marveling at how faithful and strong He was to bring you to this point. You thought that you were finally out of the valley and about to experience the fullness and blessing of Heaven on Earth. So naturally, when Jesus told you, "Ok, head this way now," you didn't hesitate a moment. You emphatically and ecstatically replied, "Yes Lord! I'll go wherever you say!" And then, all of a sudden, you find yourself in the middle of the ocean—waves swelling, winds gusting, thunder crashing. And you can't help but think, where is Jesus? He told you to go this way, but you can't see Him anywhere. The only thing you can see is the 50-foot wave in front of you about to capsize your boat and bring your life to a screeching halt.

Why do storms seem to happen right after the spiritual

mountain top? Why do tough times tend to follow the victories? A more realistic question, (if we're being completely honest) is why would Jesus lead us into another valley after we followed him all the way up the mountain? There can be many different answers to this question. But, the key observation from this story is this: storms often happen immediately after great spiritual victories. We don't always know why, but if we can simply understand this truth, it will shift our perspective greatly during the storm. Rather than asking, "God, *why* are You letting me go through this?", you can ask, "God, *what* are You trying to teach me through this?".

Why storms happen depends specifically upon where you are at in life. This exact situation happened to me at a very important and specific time in my life. Quite honestly, if this experience hadn't happened, I don't know that I would be where I am today. God taught me so much about myself and Himself through the events of my storm that it has shaped the foundation of my faith as it stands today. During the storm, all of my logic failed. I was left with just two options: trust God entirely, or abandon my faith completely. Would I trust that the same God who allowed me to go through this storm would have not only an escape from the storm, but a purpose for it? Or, would I grow cold and resentful towards the God who allowed me to experience this pain and hardship?

Storms come in all different shapes and sizes, and happen to all different kinds of people. What matters most is, when you come out on the other side, are you the same person you were when you stepped in the boat?

CHAPTER 2

BEFORE MY STORM

The year was 2012. I was 21 at the time, and life was as thrilling as it had ever been. I married my high school sweetheart in March of that year. March is a wild card month in Northeast Ohio; the weather can be anywhere from frigid and snow covered to sunny with a high of 75. Well, March 24th of 2012 just happened to be absolutely beautiful. It was warm, but not humid (as most warm Ohio days are). The apple blossom trees at the church were in full bloom, lining the parking lot with clouds of white, contrasting with the bright green grass. It truly couldn't have been a more beautiful spring day for me to say "I Do" to the love of my life.

We recited our own personal vows to each other. Mine were in the form of a song, partly because I loved writing music, but also because I knew it would make her cry. Don't misunderstand, I don't get morbid enjoyment from seeing my wife cry. My wife is the sweetest, most tenderhearted woman in the world. But, she's not a crier. One of the subtle things that I love most about her is how she abandons this natural personality trait when her heart is completely full of love and passion. She overflows with emotion. That's how I know she loves me. As I sang my heart's desire for her into that old church microphone and strummed along with the melody on my friend's Martin acoustic guitar, I could see out of the corner of my eye a couple of tears running down her cheek. She knew I loved her, and I knew she loved me. We were both 21, getting married in the church that I had grown up in since I was born. How could anything in life ever go wrong? What circumstance could possibly test the love that we both had for each other, built on the faith and love that we mutually had for our God?

After our honeymoon to Cancun, we moved into our new apartment. Life was good. We lived across the road from the church, which was convenient, because I spent every free second that I could spare there. We had a decent-sized savings account, considering we were just 21 years old. I was a pharmacy technician at a local supermarket, while she was a receptionist at a small podiatrist's office. Neither of us went to college. We had what we needed and could usually afford to buy what we wanted, or at least we could save up for it in a relatively short amount of time.

I liked my job, for the most part. Well, I liked pharmacology in general. I didn't enjoy working in retail pharmacy, as many people don't, simply because it was stressful. A small amount of the time I was doing something I enjoyed like billing, or data entry, or actually counting out prescriptions and filling the orders. Most of the time I was answering the phone, or working the cash register, or getting yelled at by a customer because their state-funded insurance didn't cover nicotine patches. It was a stressful job. But, I was working in an air-conditioned room in khaki pants and a button-up shirt. It was better than lying on my back, fixing rusty rocker panels on old cars at the body shop, as I had previously done.

I was the worship leader of the young adult ministry at our church. I served on the worship team on Sunday mornings as well, and I served anywhere and everywhere that I could. I grew up in church, and I just loved being there and serving God. I was also going through a two-year ministry training course at our church, which was a pre-requisite to going to Bible college. So, I would count pills by day, do ministry by night, and learn how to be a good husband in between.

That was a fun year. Everything was new, things were going fairly smooth, and I enjoyed just about everything in my life. It's really easy to serve God when life is going well, isn't it? I never found it hard to read my Bible, or pray, or serve at church up to this point in my life. Why wouldn't I? I had a good life, and God was a huge part of that. Why wouldn't I worship Him, and serve Him, and do everything I could to grow in my relationship with Him?

All of that was about to come to a climax in November of

2012.

HERE AM I, SEND ME

Before November of 2012, I had felt God calling me to be a pastor. That short statement deserves explanation, because so many people believe so many different things about what it means to be "called by God". But really, what I mean by that is I just wanted to be a pastor. That's all. There were no burning bushes or damp fleeces. I just simply desired to do ministry vocationally. And that's a good start, according to the Bible.

> *1 Timothy 3:1 This is a true saying, If a man desire the office of a bishop, he desireth a good work.*

I was 16 years old when I first felt this desire. Again, it wasn't anything deeply spiritual. At least, to me it wasn't. Ask any church kid who has grown up going to youth group every week since 6th grade if he thinks it would be cool to be a youth pastor, and I assure you that the majority would respond with a resounding "Yah bro!" 16-year-olds think of buying nerf guns, talking in front of people, hosting sleep-overs, and planning summer camps. Of course Youth Pastor would be a fun occupation! 16-year-olds don't think about counseling suicidal teens, sleepless nights, church politics, and empathetic heartache.

And, admittedly, I was a typical 16-year-old church kid. But, there was something else there, and I just couldn't put my finger on it. Something else in my heart that wanted to serve people. That wanted to love the unlovable. That wanted to preach God's

Word with conviction and passion to a world that needs to hear it. And I couldn't shake that. So, when I graduated high school, I pursued training and education in ministry and theology. My pastors trained me and taught me the Bible. They afforded me the opportunity to do ministry and to try new things. They allowed me to fail and showed me how to learn from my mistakes. They taught me how to study the Bible and showed me how to rightly divide the scriptures so that I could feed myself. I was falling in love with God's Word, as well as ministry.

And then, November came. Each fall, our church would host an annual missions conference. The purpose of this conference was to remind ourselves of the importance the Great Commission, and that we all have a part in it. Whether we, ourselves, go to the uttermost, or we partner with those who go by supporting them financially and prayerfully, the church must make every effort to not only reach those in our neighborhood, but across the globe. Each year we would have guest missionaries come in and preach or share their ministries with us. It always fascinated me to hear the stories of men and women who were brave enough to leave everything they know and love behind, to cross the world and live in an unfamiliar culture, just so that they could share the gospel with strangers.

We would also have a guest preacher for the main evening sessions. 800 or more people crowded into the sanctuary, eager to hear the guest preacher speak what the Lord had laid on his heart. God always moved and spoke to convicted men's and women's hearts. The Holy Spirit never failed to bring to our remembrance the importance of missions, supporting missions, praying for missions, and participating in missions.

WHATEVER, WHENEVER, WHEREVER

God did something special in my heart that year; He called me. I know I said that I felt the Lord calling me when I was 16, but this was different. God wanted a yes or a no. He didn't want my teenage response of "Oh, that would be cool!" What he wanted was for me to be all in, or all out. I don't remember every detail of what the preacher spoke about that year. I remember Him preaching about how God's plan in the Old Testament to reach the world was for the world to come to the temple and meet God there. He then went on to preach that New Testament believers are the temple on earth today, and with the Holy Spirit living inside of us, God's plan to reach the world is for us to meet them where they are. "We (the church) are the temple with feet!" I distinctly remember him saying. How true that is.

But it wasn't one specific quote or Bible verse that grabbed hold of my heart at that conference. It was simply God speaking to me through His Word, the Holy Spirit, and the preaching to lead me to a jumping point—a point of no return. I remember on the last night of the conference, when the worship band was playing the final song, I couldn't contain myself any longer. I knew that God was calling me to more than I had ever planned for my life. I didn't know if He was calling me to be a missionary specifically, but it didn't matter. He was calling me to be all-in. I wasn't all-in before this moment. I was "kind-of" in. I was in if it meant having a cool Youth Pastor gig at a comfortable church. It was a conditional "in". God told me that night, "My love for you is unconditional. Will you trust me unconditionally?"

The former pastor of my church used to say it this way, "Have you surrendered yourself to be used by God for Whatever, Whenever, and Wherever?" I could honestly say that before November of 2012 I was not. But, during the last song, on the last night of that missions conference, I was determined to be. I went up to the altar, kneeled down, and wept my eyes out. I asked God to forgive me for not surrendering all of my life to Him before. I told Him that regardless of the circumstances, I was all-in for whatever He had planned for me, whenever He wanted, and wherever He desired. That was it. Kneeling on the burgundy-carpeted steps of my church, I accepted God's calling on my life.

I went back to the pew where my wife's parents had been sitting. Brooke was serving in the nursery that night and wasn't in the service. My mother-in-law, a loving, tenderhearted woman, grabbed me and gave me a hug. Wiping away tears I told her, "I'm sorry."

"What for?", she replied.

"I have to take your daughter away from you," I said, looking her in the eyes. She understood exactly what I meant. She knew God was calling me to ministry, and she knew God was probably calling us to missions. She smiled, holding back tears, and replied simply, "I know, I know." My life would never be the same after that moment.

Struggling with the Possibility

Dr. Clifford Clark once said, "Not everyone is called to be a missionary, but everyone should struggle with the possibility." I have that quote written inside the front cover of my Bible. I heard it at a missions conference in Kansas City, Missouri once. I go to a lot of missions conferences. I try to share this quote with as many youth and young adults as I can, because I've never heard anything so simple, yet so profound at the same time. How does anyone know they are supposed to be a missionary? Well, at one point in their life, they actually considered the possibility that God would want them to be a missionary.

It sounds so simple, but it is so profound. God desires every believer to be a part of His global mission. He left us with His Great Commission, desiring us to go to the ends of the Earth and preach the gospel to everyone we could, making disciples of all nations. And regardless of your geographic location, you should be involved in evangelism and disciple-making. If you live your life regularly participating in those two things, does it really seem like a long-shot that God would call you to change your address and do that somewhere else? It's not as crazy as you might have thought. It's simply the moving of the Holy Spirit to reach the ends of the earth with the Gospel.

This is where I was at in my life as 2012 came to a close. I was on the top of the world! I felt God call me to prepare for a life of ministry and missions, and I responded "Yes" whole-heartedly. God was so real to me right then—not that He wasn't before. I accepted Christ as my Savior at the age of 10 years old, in the same church, during a communion service. God showed me through the preaching of His Word that He wanted a personal relationship with me. And for the next decade or so, I walked with Him and grew in my relationship with Him. But this was different. I felt God speaking directly to my heart in a way I had never known before. I felt like the disciples must have felt after seeing Jesus feed thousands of people with a couple of fish and loaves of bread. Yes, I knew Jesus, but now His power had been manifested in such a brilliant and personal way that it truly resonated within me like never before. God was showing me just a glimpse of the calling He had for my life, and I was anxious to get started.

Just as the disciples must have gleefully jumped on to the boat "straightway" after the miracle of Jesus in Matthew 14, I was willing to do whatever Jesus asked of me. I would have quit my job, sold everything, and moved to anywhere in the world at that point. God was drawing me to closer communion with Him, and I was allowing the Potter to begin to mold me in whatever way He saw fit. I don't know what the disciples expected to experience after getting in that boat, but I bet it wasn't the almost immediate storm they encountered. I certainly wasn't expecting what was lying ahead for me. All I knew was that Jesus told me to go "over there", so that's where I was going. That is what the disciples were doing as well. Jesus told them to go over to Gennesaret, and they were obeying. If God has told you to do something, and you are obeying, then you are right in the center of His will. Regardless of what happens, that is the safest place you can be.

More often than not, we get fixated on the destination and are inconvenienced by the journey. I remember riding in my parents' minivan with my younger brother and sister on our way to Myrtle Beach when I was a child. I was incredibly young, but that nine-hour drive to the beach was absolutely awful! I could barely stand being hauled up in that van with my annoying younger siblings for all that time. I just wanted to be at the beach!

Can you relate? Modern, western culture has aided in warping our mindset to be impatient and results-driven. Who cares about the process—I want it faster, quicker, cheaper, and easier! But quality, flawless, one-of-a-kind pottery is not manufactured on an assembly line. It is kneaded slowly and crafted gently by a caring potter who molds the clay into the shape he desires it to be. Have you ever watched a potter work? He dips his hands into the water and slowly pushes on the clay as the spinning wheel shapes it, one rotation after another. It takes patience, pressure, and time. This type of a thing cannot be rushed! And neither can God's preparing of your life as He is fashioning you into the vessel He desires you to be for the plan that He has for you. It's not always fun, but the process of preparation is vital in your life. The journey is just as important as the destination. And the journey to Gennesaret might just be more memorable for you than your arrival.

CHAPTER 3

THE STORM STRIKES

A storm is an event that disturbs our transportation from where we are to where we are headed. The disciples in Matthew 14 certainly had been halted from all forward momentum. Their journey had come to a screeching stop, and their demeanor had changed.

> Matthew 14:26 *And when the disciples saw him walking on the sea, they were troubled, saying, It is a spirit; and they cried out for fear.*

We'll get to Jesus walking on the water later. For now, notice the disciple's reactions to Jesus. 1) They were troubled, 2) They thought Jesus was a spirit, 3) and they cried out for fear. This all happens in reaction to seeing Jesus. This storm had completely knocked out their personal navigation systems. They didn't know which way was up!

IT'S A GHOST!

First of all, if seeing Jesus makes you "troubled", you are either on the wrong side of the Second Coming, or you've forgotten what He looks like. The Bible says that Jesus brings peace, not trouble.

> *Philippians 4:7 And the peace of God, which passeth all understanding, shall keep your hearts and minds through Christ Jesus.*

So why are the disciples troubled? They have been so focused on the storm around them, they don't recognize Jesus in the storm. That is made evident when they say, "It is a spirit". Notice that "spirit" isn't capitalized here. That is because the disciples are not saying that Jesus is THE Spirit. Jesus is God manifested in flesh (1Timothy 3:16). He is the "word made flesh" (John 1:14), and He is one part of the Godhead (1 John 5:7). He is not THE Holy Spirit here, because the Spirit had not yet come (John 14:26, 15:26, 16:7). This Jesus, walking on the water, is the Man, Christ Jesus (1Timothy 2:5). What the disciples thought they saw was "a" spirit (lower case "s"). In other words, they thought He was a ghost! They didn't recognize Him. That is why they then "cried out for fear".

Granted, it was nighttime, and it was dark. They saw a figure of a man walking on the water, and they thought it was a ghost.

Can you imagine the thoughts running through their heads? "Man, this storm is going to kill us! The waves are massive, we are taking on water, and we can't go anywhere! Wait—what's that on the port side? Is that... Is that a ghost? Great, not only do we have to worry about these waves, now we've got ghosts too!"

I'm not trying to come down too hard on them. I understand where they're coming from. But, why didn't they recognize Jesus? Or, why did their minds jump to the conclusion that a ghost was on the water, rather than Jesus? I think the answer is because the storm at hand had made them lose their focus. I think they were so focused on the storm they had forgotten all about Jesus.

We do the same thing, don't we? When we are surprised by a giant storm in our life, often immediately after great spiritual victory, we completely forget about Jesus. We forget that He told us to come here. It quickly becomes "all hands on deck!", and our entire focus is shifted to the task at hand: survival. When we go into survival mode, Jesus blends into the chaos surrounding us rather than sticking out like the beacon and life preserver that He is.

That's what happened to me, too. I completely lost all sight of Jesus in my storm. I completely forgot how He had led me through all the amazing victories in my life just prior. In fact, I used those victories to cry out to God in anger, as if to say, "God, remember all the great stuff I just did for you? How could you abandon me and let me go through this?" I would equate this to the disciples "crying out in fear". It wasn't a sensible thing to think. In fact, it was quite selfish. But when you are in the center of the storm, you lose sight of sensibility and logic. You look out on the water, like the disciples, and think Jesus is a ghost. How did this happen? How could I have gotten to this place, after all God brought me through just a couple of months ago?

At the close of 2012, I was on the spiritual mountain top, ready for whatever Jesus told me to do. He had given me direction, and I had boarded the ship and started my journey to Gennesaret. It didn't take long for me to encounter the storm on the sea.

PROVE IT

I call 2013 my year of "Prove It". At the close of 2012, I told God that I was "all-in". I would do what He wanted me to do, I would go where He wanted me to go, and I would do it all whenever He wanted me to. God's response was, "Prove it." The storm would simply be the instrument God used to test me.

In January of 2013, I had scheduled an appointment with my family doctor. I had some annoying symptoms, like acid reflux, that were really bothering me. I was hoping he could write me a few prescriptions, and I would be on my way. Luckily, my doctor wasn't as quick to write a script as I thought he'd be. He looked at all my symptoms and he asked me, "Kale, you don't drink alcohol or use cigarettes or drugs, right?"

I said, "Of course not. Never have, never will."

He replied, "Everything you're experiencing, by itself, is a common problem. But, you aren't doing anything to cause any of them, especially all of them at the same time. Just to be safe, I want you to go see a specialist and make sure everything is ok."

Wow, I thought. A specialist? I was only 22 years old. What could possibly be wrong with me that some Nexium couldn't fix? I was a bit worried, but I shrugged it off. When you are a young adult, you feel invincible, like nothing serious could ever affect you. Well, I was about to have my whole world turned upside down within a month.

On a side note, just a couple of days before this doctor's appointment, things at work had become very stressful. A coworker had been fired the day before my appointment because she had stolen $10,000 worth of gift cards. That's not an easy thing to do. This person would have had to stay down at the cash register and scan gift cards, activate them, and pocket them without anyone noticing—for a while. When all of this happened, our entire pharmacy couldn't believe it. We were all a bit shaken up, especially since important corporate suits had begun investigating our pharmacy. Private interviews, security tapes, you name it. Everything we said and did was under scrutiny, and it felt like I was living under a magnifying glass.

Two days later, another coworker was fired. This was the day after my doctor's appointment. It was unfortunate, because this coworker was let go due to a simple protocol error. It wasn't malicious; it was just an innocent mistake. It could have happened to any of us. But, since we had corporate staring at our every move, this mistake didn't slip by unnoticed, and this person was the second to be fired in a span of two days. Now the stress was setting in. Everyone, including me, began to worry about everything they had ever done in the last couple of months. What would they find on the video tapes? Had I forgotten something? We all feared for our jobs, and the minute hand on the clock seemed to move ever slower as the days went on.

During this work chaos, I went to see the specialist. I had never seen a specialist before, so I didn't know what was going to happen. Basically, when the doctors don't know what is wrong with you, and they want to find out, they start scheduling a myriad of different kinds of tests, scans, and blood work. I had insurance through my job at the pharmacy, but it wasn't good insurance. As a 22-year-old, I didn't see the need in paying for expensive insurance premiums with low deductibles that I never used. As I began to realize how expensive this diagnosis was going to be, I started to stress. This anxiety multiplied quickly because of the stress at work. I began to think, if I lose my job, I won't have insurance. How will I pay for all of this? The waves were beginning to beat against the ship.

Do you know what a Barium Swallow test is? Oh man, they're awful. You have to drink several large cups of thick, chalky-tasting barium, one right after another. This compound they make you drink makes your esophagus and stomach show up really well during an X-ray, and they can see any abnormalities. I did that in the beginning of February. I also had many different kinds of blood work done, so much so I thought that maybe it would be easier for the nurse if I just tattooed a target on the inside of my elbow that said, "Stick me here!"

Next, the specialist ordered a colonoscopy and an endoscopy. He wanted to take a look at me from the inside. This was a big deal for me, because I had never had a procedure of this nature before. It was almost like going in for surgery in that you have the gown on, they put you under with anesthesia… the whole nine yards. I was scared, but I didn't know what to expect yet. I didn't know that the wind was starting to really pick up.

The specialist told me after the procedure that he thought he saw evidence of something called Crohn's Disease. He said he wasn't positive though, so he ordered a biopsy and wanted me to get more blood work. Of course. That was the story of my life the last couple of weeks. But this Crohn's Disease caught me off guard. I had no idea what that was, and I had never heard of it. The doctor told me that it was an auto-immune disease, closely related to Ulcerative Colitis, that causes inflammation in the intestines. It's a tricky disease, because it can manifest itself in many different ways and symptoms in different people. I asked him what the cure was. I can still hear his response in my head today. He said, "There is none". He continued to tell me that we don't know much about why it happens, or what causes it. He said you just have to find the right treatment that works for you and hope you can get it into remission.

The official diagnosis came on February 28, 2013; I had Crohn's Disease. The symptoms I was having were not just simple problems to be solved with over-the-counter medications, they were alerts from my body that something much more serious was going on. Something severe. Something that I would never had dreamt a 22-year-old guy would have to deal with. The storm had begun to rage.

In March, the doctor began searching for the correct treatment for me. This was an arduous process of trial and error, because the doctor didn't know how my body would react to each medication. One medication did nothing. Another one seemed to be working, but then reacted adversely to my body, beginning to give me pancreatitis. That was incredibly painful. Every medication we tried involved waiting and more blood work. It wasn't until May of that year that the doctor found a medication that seemed to be working. The first five months of 2013 were consumed with stress, worry, pain, and doctor's bills.

Can I be honest with you? This was the hardest five-month stretch of my entire life up to that point. I was scared, angry, and at times, hopeless. I had lost a lot of my joy. I was in and out of hospitals. I was in and out of crippling abdominal pain and symptoms that come along with that. The medical bills were beginning to pile up on the kitchen table, and with every check I wrote our small savings account was dwindling. Everything in my life had come to a screeching halt. I had ceased all forward momentum, and I had begun toiling in rowing.

I was actually angry at God a lot. I would pray these incredibly honest prayers to God, asking Him how he could let all of this happen to me. I remember reminding Him that He was the one who had told me to get on this boat, and I was just obeying *His* orders! I was going the direction *He* had told me to go. He asked me to be all-in, and I told Him that I was. Why in the world would He let me, His faithful, obedient servant, go through this horrible storm?

THE STORM STRIKES

I had lost sight of Jesus in the storm. Like the disciples, I didn't even recognize that Jesus was right there beside me. Even though I felt like my prayers were falling on deaf ears, I was right in the center of God's will. And even though that happened to also be right in the center of an incredibly difficult storm, He was right there with me.

CHAPTER 4

JESUS IN THE STORM

When we left the disciples, they couldn't recognize who Jesus was. They thought He was a spirit, and cried out for fear. All of this was because they were focused on the storm and not the God of creation.

But, I want us to back up in the story just a bit. Right before we see the disciples' reaction to Jesus, we see Jesus enter the story.

> Matthew 14:24-26
> 24 But the ship was now in the midst of the sea, tossed with waves: for the wind was contrary.
> 25 And in the fourth watch of the night Jesus went unto them, walking on the sea.
> 26 And when the disciples saw him walking on the sea, they were troubled, saying, It is a spirit; and they cried out for fear.

Two words couldn't possibly have more meaning in this situation. "Jesus went". The disciples are battling for their lives in a brutal storm, and "Jesus went" unto them. It is Jesus Himself who seeks out the terrified disciples who are toiling in rowing. It is Jesus Himself who takes the initiative to move towards His disciples. The disciples might be wondering where Jesus is, but it is Jesus Himself who is going to them!

Christian, when you are going through the ringer and the waves are ramming the sides of your ship, just remember this: Jesus is coming to you. Yes, it may seem as though all hope is lost, and everyone has abandoned you, and there is no light at the end of the tunnel. But, Jesus is coming to you. He is moving toward you. It doesn't matter that you've abandoned all lines of communication through prayer and reading God's Word, He is coming to you. It doesn't matter that you probably won't recognize Him when He gets there, but He is coming to you.

GOOD EVENING!

To understand when Jesus went to them, you must understand that the Hebrew clock is not the same as ours today. First of all, the Hebrew "day" begins at sunset. The evening always comes before the morning for a 24-hour Hebrew day. You can see this in the Scripture during the creation week in Genesis 1. Over and over again, day after day, "and the *evening* and the morning" were that day. In a western mindset, the morning is what begins the day. We might say something like "and the *morning* and the evening were the second day". But that's not how God works, and it's not

51

how the Hebrew clock works. The evening comes first each day.

Generally, Hebrew "night-time" is from about 6:00 pm to 6:00 am, and "day-time" is from 6:00 am to 6:00 pm. You can use this to understand at what time different things happen in the Bible, and especially in the Gospels. The "third hour of the day" in Acts 2:15 would be about 9:00 am, which makes the passage make even more sense, considering Peter was arguing against false claims that men who had received the Holy Spirit were actually just drunk. Peter essentially says, "No way! It's only 9:00 am. That doesn't make sense".

So, the Hebrew "night-time" is a 12-hour span from about 6:00 pm to 6:00 am. In the New Testament, that time was separated into four sections called "watches." Jesus went to the disciples during the "fourth watch of the night." So, this would have been the last 25 percent of the "night-time" before sunrise. Or, somewhere between 3:00 am and 6:00 am.[1]

Why does that matter? Timing is everything. Jesus comes on the scene right at the very end of the night. He didn't come in right when the storm started and command the seas to stop swelling. He didn't show up right when the first raindrop fell or when the first clap of thunder roared. No, Jesus came right in the nick of time. He allowed the disciples to go through this storm before saving the day. He allowed them to have their faith tested, to see how they would fare. It's no wonder James says:

---

[1] "Determining the Hebrew Hour," Torah Calendar, accessed December 12, 2019, http://torahcalendar.com/HOUR.asp

James 1:2-4
2 My brethren, count it all joy when ye fall into divers temptations;
3 Knowing this, that the trying of your faith worketh patience.
4 But let patience have her perfect work, that ye may be perfect and entire, wanting nothing.

The storms and tribulations have a purpose, but that isn't what we want to hear when we are stuck in the middle of one. If we can keep the perspective that God is allowing this to happen to shape and mold us for His plan, we can make it through the storm better. It won't be easier, but maybe when Jesus comes walking up to us, we won't scream, "Ah, a ghost!" Because we'll be waiting for Him.

WALKING ON THE SEA

Notice *how* Jesus came to them. His "mode of transportation". He "went unto them, *walking on the sea.*" Unbeknownst to the frantic disciples in the ship, Jesus was displaying His power and authority by walking to them on top of the very sea that was trying to consume them. What power! What omnipotence! With every stride, Jesus not only defied the laws of physics, but He manifested His strength and supremacy by stepping on the very waves that were the source of the disciple's travail! He trampled underfoot what was causing their near-death experience. Jesus was establishing His prominence and preeminence over nature, and the disciples were too afraid to notice. Perhaps if they were focused on their Lord, rather than the storm, they would have noticed the still waters under His feet, as opposed to the roaring waves around them.

Christian, in the midst of your storm, Jesus is Lord. He is King. With every step He takes, He tramples underfoot the very problems that have your entire life in upheaval. Don't forget what He has *already* conquered to bring you eternal life! The man, Christ Jesus, conquered sin and the grave to deliver you from Hell. He holds the keys to death and Hell, and He will one day yet future trample underfoot the god of this world, Satan himself. Christ has overcome the world! Yet, how quickly we forget His power and omnipotence when the waves rise up around us.

As Jesus approaches the ship, the disciples cry out in fear. They are caught up in the atmosphere of the storm, consumed with terror. Their reaction to Christ is threefold: 1) they were troubled, 2) they said, "It is a spirit", 3) they cried out for fear. Those are three very specific reactions. Notice, these aren't their reactions to the storm; no, these are their reactions to seeing Jesus! Certainly, the storm has had an effect on their senses and their actions are irrational at this point, although they probably seem completely rational to themselves.

Three Rational Responses to Three Irrational Reactions

Luckily for the disciples, Jesus has three rational responses to their three irrational reactions. Notice how Jesus greets the toiling men:

> *Matthew 14:27 But straightway Jesus spake unto them, saying, Be of good cheer; it is I; be not afraid.*

Straightway, or immediately, Jesus spoke to them and said 1) "Be of good cheer", 2) "It is I", 3) "Be not afraid". That is not just the sympathetic voice of a consoling father trying to soothe his crying infant. No, these are very specific responses aimed at the heart of the three irrational reactions the disciples had when they saw Jesus.

1. TROUBLED? BE OF GOOD CHEER!

First, the disciples were troubled. Jesus' response? "Be of good cheer!" There is no need to be troubled at the presence of Jesus. Of course, the storm is troubling, but the presence of God is reassuring. And Jesus cries out to the troubled men, "Be of good cheer!"

You may think, how in the world could I be of good cheer at this point in my life? This storm has all but sunk my little ship, and water is flooding in on every side. Christian, are you troubled? Have you given up hope? Jesus' response to you right now is, "Be of good cheer!" Not because the storm is cheerful, but because Jesus is there with you, and He has overcome.

> *John 16:33 These things I have spoken unto you, that in me ye might have peace. In the world ye shall have tribulation: but be of good cheer; I have overcome the world.*

Of course, the world will bring tribulation, but Jesus has overcome the world! And as a result, you can be of good cheer. The same Jesus who has overcome the grave is standing beside you in the storm, waiting for you to quit flailing about so that He can bring you through it. Notice the juxtaposition of the world and Christ in John 16:33. In Christ, you can have peace. In the world, you will have tribulation. Because of who Christ is and what he has done for you, you can have peace!

Philippians 4:6-7
6 Be careful for nothing; but in every thing by prayer and supplication with thanksgiving let your requests be made known unto God.
7 And the peace of God, which passeth all understanding, shall keep your hearts and minds through Christ Jesus.

Through faith and prayer, God will provide you with peace. But not just any peace, the "peace of God, which passeth all understanding." He will give you a peace that doesn't make sense! Do you know what that means? It means He will give you peace despite your circumstances. Even though the raging storm surrounds you, you can have peace. Peace that Jesus is there. Peace that He has overcome. Peace that: "There hath no temptation taken you but such as is common to man: but God is faithful, who will not suffer you to be tempted above that ye are able; but will with the temptation also make a way to escape, that ye may be able to bear it." (1 Corinthians 10:13)

People may even look at you and wonder, how could you possibly be so peaceful during this time in your life? They may look at you in amazement as they see the monsoon beating down on your life, only to see you basking in the peace of who Jesus is. It really is a "peace that passeth all understanding" because, from a human perspective, it makes no logical sense at all. But from

God's perspective, you're placing your faith in the person of Christ to bring you through it all. Not only is that comforting, but it's sustaining. Relying solely on Christ during the storm will bring you peace, comfort, and cheer that sustains you all the way to the other side. That's why Jesus responds to the disciples' troubled demeanor with the admonition "be of good cheer."

2. SEEING SPIRITS? NO, IT IS I!

Second, the disciples said, "It is a spirit", referring to Jesus. His response? "It is I". Notice, He doesn't say His name. Why should He? They should know exactly who He is, for Jesus says in John 10:4 that "...the sheep follow him: for they know his *voice*." Christ simply calls out to the disciples with His voice—the very same voice that called them by name to drop what they were doing and follow Him. It is His voice that the sheep should know.

In John 20, after Jesus has resurrected, He appears to Mary Magdalene outside of the sepulcher. Mary doesn't recognize Jesus and actually thinks that He is the gardener. We must be fair to Mary though, for Jesus obviously looked a bit different after the resurrection. But, all of that aside, how does Mary finally come to realize who was standing in front of her?

> *John 20:16 Jesus saith unto her, Mary. She turned herself, and saith unto him, Rabboni; which is to say, Master.*

When Jesus said her name, she recognized Him. All He had to do was utter her name with His vocal cords, and she quickly came to her senses. Maybe that's because John 10:3 says that "he calleth his own sheep by name."

But, in the disciple's scenario, He doesn't call them each individually by name. Surely, He has in the past. But that is not the specific issue at hand here. The issue is that the disciples didn't recognize Jesus and mistook him for an apparition. Jesus simply responds with "It is I". Notice, He doesn't refute the irrational claim that He is, by implication, an evil spirit. No, His only response to this irrational fear amidst a raging sea of complications is to verify His identity through a very specific word choice.

Now, this may seem to be an ambiguous way of confirming one's identity. But we've already seen that Jesus' *voice* is what the disciples should recognize. Furthermore, Jesus picks His words very carefully. "It is I…"

A "few" years before this storm in Matthew 14, there was a man named Moses tending sheep on the backside of a desert. This man was a fugitive of the law, hiding out with his father-in-law because he had murdered an Egyptian. Something caught Moses' attention one day, when a bush was burning but wasn't consumed by the flames. When he turned to get a better look, who else but God begins to speak to him from the fire. He tells Moses of His plan to deliver Israel from the bondage of the Egyptians, and that He wants Moses to go and do it. Moses will give several excuses as to why he is not the right man for the job, but notice what God says when Moses asserts that Israel will want to know just *who* this God is that wants to deliver them:

Exodus 3:13-14
13 And Moses said unto God, Behold, when I come unto the children of Israel, and shall say unto them, The God of your fathers hath sent me unto you; and they shall say to me, What is his name? what shall I say unto them?
14 And God said unto Moses, I AM THAT I AM: and he said, Thus shalt thou say unto the children of Israel, I AM hath sent me unto you.

God tells Moses that I AM will deliver Israel. The God of their fathers, Abraham, Isaac, Jacob... His name is I AM. Not only does He deliver Israel through Moses, but He continually provides in miraculous fashion as He brings Israel out of Egypt, through the wilderness, across the Jordan, and into Canaan to defeat the enemies of the land and deliver it as an inheritance to His people. That's who I AM is.

That's who Jesus is. Jesus is equal with the Father. He is 100 percent deity, and He tells Israel that in no uncertain terms in John 10:30 when He says, "I and my Father are one." Jesus is I AM. In fact, in John 18 when Judas is bringing a band of men to apprehend Jesus, He asks the men, "Whom seek ye?" They answer, "Jesus of Nazareth". Jesus then replies, "I am he". Guess what happens next?

John 18:6 As soon then as he had said unto them, I am he, they went backward, and fell to the ground.

Jesus displays His power and absolute deity by simply saying (with His *voice*) I AM he. At the utterance of His name, the men fall down on the ground. Jesus is the great I AM!

I believe He is reminding His troubled disciples of just exactly who He is as they battle it out in the storm. By saying "It is I", it's almost as if He is saying, "Remember me? The One who called you all to be my disciples? The One who has done amazing miracles? The One who you just watched feed 10,000 people with a couple pieces of bread and a few fish? Remember me?"

Christian, do you remember Him? Have you lost all sense of memory in the storm? Do you remember that He is the One who brought you out of the kingdom of darkness and translated you into the kingdom of His dear Son? Do you remember what He did when He picked you up out of the miry clay and made you alive? Do you remember how He quickened you, and chose you, and adopted you?

How about this; do you remember that He is the I AM? Do you remember that this Jesus is the same God who parted the Red Sea and brought Israel across on dry ground? Do you remember that He is the same God who rained manna from Heaven to feed the nation of Israel in the wilderness? Do you remember that He is the same God who brought down the walls of Jericho, defeated Goliath for David, stopped the lion's mouths for Daniel, and was *in the fire* with Hananiah, Mishael, and Azariah? Do you remember Him? Well, He is *in the storm with you*, coming towards you, and calling out to you. Do you recognize Him? Or does His presence frighten you, as it did the disciples, because you've allowed Him to blend in with the swirling circumstances around you?

He calls out, "It is I".

3. FEARFUL? BE NOT AFRAID!

Lastly, the disciples cried out for fear. Jesus' response? "Be not afraid." What seems like a fairly obvious statement is actually a profound assessment of their current state. Why are they afraid? Remember, Jesus isn't necessarily referring to the storm here. The disciples "cried out for fear" at the sight of Jesus in the storm. They are afraid of Jesus, because they don't recognize who He is! So, after Jesus identifies Himself, he says "be not afraid." He is specifically addressing their lack of faith in who He is.

That all starts with forgetting about Jesus when the storm began. If they would have remembered that Jesus was the one who sent them on this journey and promised to meet them on the other side, maybe they wouldn't have lost all hope when this storm hit. Not to dismiss the magnitude of the storm, but the disciples forgot about Jesus' deity and power in less than a night. That is an incredibly rapid decrease in faith! So much so, that when Jesus shows up on the scene, not only do they not recognize Him, but they respond with cries of fear. That is a surefire manifestation of just how much faith they currently have—none.

Can you relate? I know that it's easy to pick on the disciples here, but when was the last time your circumstances overwhelmed you to such a degree that your lack of faith in God to provide and sustain you was manifested outwardly through fear? Fear is a good indicator of our faith level. And, just for clarification, I'm not talking about the godly, reverential "fear of the Lord" the Scripture often references, that results in obedience (1 Samuel 11:7), wisdom (Psalm 111:10), knowledge (Proverbs 1:7), prolonged days (Proverbs 10:27), confidence (Proverbs 14:26), and righteousness (Proverbs 16:6). No, we're talking about the kind of fear that stems from focusing on bad circumstances rather than Christ, resulting in disobedience (Jonah), inactivity (1 Samuel 17:24), and irrational panic (the disciples here). Yes, fear is the fruit that we see clearly manifested in the moment, *but the root of the matter is our lack of faith.*

But why does our faith waiver when the storm hits? I know the practical answer, but what is the deeper answer? Why is it that we, of all people, Christians, lose sight of the big picture when our immediate scenery grows gray and thundery? Have we forgotten His promises?

> *Deuteronomy 20:1 When thou goest out to battle against thine enemies, and seest horses, and chariots, and a people more than thou, be not afraid of them: for the LORD thy God is with thee, which brought thee up out of the land of Egypt.*

This Old Testament promise to Israel is fitting, in picture, for us today. The God who brought us up out of spiritual Egypt (bondage to sin) is with us when we go out to battle against spiritual enemies (Ephesians 6:12). The exhortation? Be not afraid!

> *Joshua 1:9 Have not I commanded thee? Be strong and of a good courage; be not afraid, neither be thou dismayed: for the LORD thy God is with thee whithersoever thou goest.*

God reminds Joshua that He is the One who commanded him to go where he is going. Because of this, God exhorts him to be "strong, and of a good courage; be not afraid!" Why? "For the

LORD thy God is with thee…"

I think the disciples had forgotten that Jesus was the one who told them to take this journey in the first place; meaning, He was going to be with them wherever they went. There was no need for them to cry out for fear at the sight of Jesus. They could have, and *should* have, been relieved. But often enough when we are hit with torrential circumstances, Jesus blends into the scenery. Christian, if you are going through a storm today, can I remind you of Who it is that told you to go to the other side? The same Jesus who has previously worked miracles in your life. The same Jesus you exuberantly followed onto the ship after He gave you your marching orders. The Jesus you were willing to follow to the ends of the earth. I AM has sent you.

> *Psalm 27:1 The LORD is my light and my salvation; whom shall I fear? the LORD is the strength of my life; of whom shall I be afraid?*

> *Psalm 56:3 What time I am afraid, I will trust in thee.*

Jesus' responses to the disciples' irrational reactions are specific. It cuts to the heart of the matter and draws attention to their lack of faith. Maybe that is where you are at right now? Has the storm that you are in right now fogged up your navigation instruments so that you can't recognize Jesus coming to you, walking on the waters? Remember, you can always decide to shift your focus back to the One who calms the seas. All it takes is faith.

JOURNEY TO GENNESARET

CHAPTER 5

REFINER'S FIRE

It's been said that the purpose of the book of Job in the Bible is to show us why the righteous suffer. This analysis isn't very fair to the main character of that book though, for Job is never once told why he was suffering. God comes in at the very end of the book and asks Job a series of rhetorical questions meant to reveal just how powerful and infinite He was in comparison to Job's weakness and finiteness. Job repents of his "whining" (who would blame him though?), and God rebukes his selfish and self-righteous counselors and their folly. But, God never tells Job *why* he suffered. Now, through the recorded Scripture, we can see today that God allowed Job to suffer to glorify Himself! But, is that *sufficient*, dare I say, *edifying* to someone who is suffering through a storm of that magnitude?

Job was a righteous man, though, and at the very least had a good response to the storm he was caught in:

Job 23:10 But he knoweth the way that I take: when he hath tried me, I shall come forth as gold.

Job knew how gold was refined. As heat is added to gold, the impurities float to the surface and are scraped off. That's called the dross. Silver is refined, or "tried", in the same manner. Even though Job didn't know why he was being tried, he vowed to allow the Divine Goldsmith to scrape off the dross in his life, so that he may come through the fire more pure and holy, as He is holy.

God's Word speaks on several occasions about the idea of refining precious metals like gold and silver. He even uses this illustration when referring to His very words.

Psalm 12:6 The words of the LORD are pure words: as silver tried in a furnace of earth, purified seven times.

In Proverbs, God lets us know that this process of refinement is how He "tries" His people.

Proverbs 17:3 The fining pot is for silver, and the furnace for gold: but the LORD trieth the hearts.

SEARCH ME...

God's desire for His people is that they may be holy, as He is holy. God desires perfect, mature, complete Christians who have crucified the flesh and yielded their members as instruments of righteousness. He repudiates sin and the ways of this world's system, and rather than conforming to it, He calls the believer to transform their mind through His Word. If God so desires this for His children, then how else can He refine us but by turning up the heat?

David specifically asked God for refinement in his life.

Psalm 139:23-24
23 Search me, O God, and know my heart: try me, and know my thoughts:
24 And see if there be any wicked way in me, and lead me in the way everlasting.

David requested that God would search his heart, locate any impurities, and remove them. Should this not also be the desire of our hearts? If we truly wish to be conformed to the image of Christ and follow Him wherever He leads, we must voluntarily submit ourselves to the Refiner's flame. But, be careful what you wish for. If you ask God to refine you, that is exactly what He will do!

I'm not saying that Job asked the Lord for what He went through, and I'm certainly not saying that you have either. We have no evidence that the disciples personally requested that Jesus would send them through a hurricane, and no reason to think that they would want to! But, what is the common link between these stories and, hopefully, your own? It's that all of the aforementioned parties *desired* to follow God.

Now, let me take just a second to make sure you realize that I'm well aware of the principle of "sowing and reaping" found in Galatians 6. If we have sown to our flesh and made poor decisions, then we certainly will reap of our flesh! It is absolutely possible that whatever storm we are in is self-inflicted because of poor decisions and sin. I cannot personally judge your situation, nor do I want to. But, if you are anything like Job and anything like the disciples, you were probably just trying to follow the Lord as best as you can. Job continuously fended off accusations from his "friends" that his awful state was a result of his own hidden sin. Poor Job! What a way to add insult to injury. There he sat, covered from head to toe in puss-seeping boils, all of his children dead, and his friends repeatedly called him a liar for saying that he had not done anything to deserve this!

The only way of knowing the answer to this is to be honest with ourselves and look into the mirror of God's Word to "see if there be any wicked way" in us, and repent if there is. If you are experiencing a storm of circumstances as a result of your own poor choices and sinful behaviors, don't blame God for it. And you know what? Don't blame the devil either! This is a bit of a rabbit trail, so I will stick close to the path. But I have often heard people blaming Satan for their misery in life, and they have not been on Satan's radar in years! Why would Satan have to worry about a Christian who continually lives after the flesh? He wouldn't—and he doesn't.

If your current situation is a result of personal sin, just repent! Get right with God. Don't forget Christian, you are a son of God

(1 John 3:1, John 1:12), and as His son, He will chastise you if you are disobedient. As a loving father disciplines his erring child, so will our Heavenly Father correct us in order to bring us back to Himself (Proverbs 3:11-12, Hebrews 12:5-11).

Ok, let's get back to being encouraging. I'm going to assume that whatever storm you are going through as you are reading this has you baffled, much like the disciples in Matthew 14. Like Job, you aren't aware of anything you have done to warrant this cyclone of catastrophic circumstances, and you aren't quite sure why you are going through it. I know that in my personal life, I didn't understand at all why God was allowing me to go through the storm I have shared with you. But, if you are anything like I was, or Job, or the disciples, you probably desire to follow God. Am I right? Believer, if this is true, then perhaps God is turning up the heat so he can purify you and use you for greater things than you are currently capable of.

VESSELS OF HONOR

In 2 Timothy, God speaks through the Apostle Paul about vessels of honor and dishonor.

> *2 Timothy 2:20-21*
> *20 But in a great house there are not only vessels of gold and of silver, but also of wood and of earth; and some to honour, and some to dishonour.*
> *21 If a man therefore purge himself from these, he shall be a vessel unto honour, sanctified, and meet for the master's use, and prepared unto every good work.*

The vessels of honor are made of gold and silver, and the vessels of dishonor are made of wood and earth (or clay of some sort). A vessel is simply a container. A vessel holds things. A vessel is filled with something. It is used for a purpose.

Now, one thing is clear here, and that is both of these types of vessels are "in" the house. So, both of these types of containers are representative of Christians. The vessels of dishonor cannot be lost people, for they are "in" the house.

In my house, we have lots of vessels, or containers. I have buckets in my garage for washing the cars. My wife has Tupperware for storing food. We have coffee cups for early morning energy, and we have trashcans for trash. We also have this large, porcelain vessel in a separate room that is used for, well, you know. See what I mean? A house has many vessels in it, and they all have different purposes. But, if a man wants to be a vessel unto honor, "sanctified, and meet for the master's use", he is desiring to be used for more than flushing away waste!

In a King's house, there are certainly many vessels. Nehemiah was the cupbearer for King Artaxerxes. He was the trusted associate of the King who would ensure that his cup was untampered with—i.e., absent of poison. Do you think that the cup that Nehemiah was entrusted to prepare for the King to drink from was made of clay or wood? I doubt it. I'm sure it was an expensive, beautifully crafted chalice made from precious metals. After all, the King of the free world isn't going to drink from a peasant's mug! But, it goes without saying that the King would need his clothes washed, baths drawn, and so forth. Those vessels would have been made of less desirable materials. Are they in the house? Yes! Do they serve a purpose? Of course! But let me ask you this, Christian: would you like to be the cup in the hand of the King, or the pot that holds dirty bath water?

If you want to be a vessel of honor, used by the King of Kings to accomplish His purposes and bring Him glory and honor and praise, then it's going to require some refining. God is going to turn up the heat in your life and see what impurities float to the top. And, if you let Him, He'll scrape off the dross time and time again. And as the Great Refiner works in you, He'll begin to see His own reflection in you more clearly.

But, let's just be honest, refining doesn't feel very nice. It's uncomfortable when the heat gets turned up. Impurities boiling to the surface is not a fun time. Dross-scraping is not an enjoyable experience. These times of trying can be incredibly painful. But, if we step back for a moment and assess the situation from a larger, more heavenly perspective, maybe we can understand that the purpose of the storm is to reveal to us those parts of our lives that need further refining. And if we can understand the purpose of the storm, maybe we can bear it just a bit better. I'm not saying it will be easier, but it will give us the hope we need to sustain us.

TRIBULATION WORKETH PATIENCE...

Consider the following scriptures which talk about trials, our expectations of them, and the results thereof.

> *1 Corinthians 10:13 There hath no temptation taken you but such as is common to man: but God is faithful, who will not*

suffer you to be tempted above that ye are able; but will with the temptation also make a way to escape, that ye may be able to bear it.

This is God's personal promise to you that whatever He allows you to go through, you are capable of bearing. If you don't think you can survive the storm you are going through, you are wrong! God says He will not allow you to be tempted above what you are able. And, He has provided a way to escape. If you had to guess, what do you think that escape is? Here's a hint: it's the Man walking on the water toward you.

Romans 5:3-5
3 And not only so, but we glory in tribulations also: knowing that tribulation worketh patience;
4 And patience, experience; and experience, hope:
5 And hope maketh not ashamed; because the love of God is shed abroad in our hearts by the Holy Ghost which is given unto us.

In this passage, God shows us that storms have a purpose. They work in us patience. Isn't that the truth? If you've ever come through a storm before, chances are God taught you to wait on Him through it. But, it doesn't stop there. Patience results in experience. Experience of life, tribulations, waiting on the Lord for deliverance, and faith. And this experience ultimately results in hope. This is the hope we need to get us through the storms in the future. Hope that God will bring us through that storm just like He brought us through this storm.

This reminds me of Joshua 4. In this chapter, the children of Israel, under the leadership of Joshua, have crossed over the Jordan river. God tells them to go back into the river and take out 12 stones from the midst of Jordan. Then He tells them to stack them up in a pile on the other side where they will spend the night. Why did God want them to do this? He tells them that the purpose of this pile of stones is to be a "sign", or a memorial, of what God has done for them. When they look upon the pile of rocks, they'll remember how God brought them across the river on dry ground. And, when their children ask them about the stones, they could share with them about God's faithfulness.

Do you have any piles of stones in your life? When you look in the rear-view mirror, can you see different memorials of all that God has done for you? Maybe this storm has made you forget all that God has done. Even if this is the first significant storm in your life since salvation, you do have one very significant pile of stones right at the beginning of your spiritual life!

> *1 Peter 1:7 That the trial of your faith, being much more precious than of gold that perisheth, though it be tried with fire, might be found unto praise and honour and glory at the appearing of Jesus Christ:*

Peter knew that the refining of our faith was important. In fact, it is supposed to result in praise and honor and glory to God at the appearing of Jesus Christ.

> *1 Peter 4:12-13*
> *12 Beloved, think it not strange concerning the fiery trial which*

is to try you, as though some strange thing happened unto you:
13 But rejoice, inasmuch as ye are partakers of Christ's
sufferings; that, when his glory shall be revealed, ye may be glad
also with exceeding joy.

I love these two verses. God tells us, don't think that it's strange when you go through a fiery trial. Why would we think this is strange, when God tells us in 2 Timothy 3:12 that "all that will live godly in Christ Jesus shall suffer persecution"? That's not a suggestion, Christian–that's a promise!

We shouldn't be surprised by storms in our life. But instead, we should rejoice! What? Why should I rejoice when I'm going through tribulation? Because you are a partaker of Christ's sufferings. No matter what we go through in life, we will never go through the pain and tribulation that He suffered for us. We can, however, partake in His sufferings when our faith is tried. And that, friends, you can find joy in.

God had a purpose for the disciples' storm. It wasn't random. It wasn't providential pain. God was working their faith and trying their hearts. Their initial reactions to Jesus in the storm were not good. How have your reactions to Jesus in the storm been? Can you relate to the disciples? Well, here's some good news: you can change your mind. You can refocus your vision. You don't have to continue stewing in the storm. You can stop looking at the waves and start focusing on Jesus. You can jump out of the boat and begin to walk towards Him.

CHAPTER 6

PETER IN THE STORM

I remember Jesus speaking to me during my storm. Even though my emotions shifted on a daily basis, rocking back and forth with the tide of the waves, one thing remained constant—my time in the word and prayer. This is the test that many Christians fail when they are going through a storm. Many people will become so frustrated with their circumstances that they actually stop reading their Bible and praying completely. It's as if they have become so mad at God for the storm they are going through, that they think giving God the 'silent treatment' will make matters better!

Have you ever done this? Maybe this is where you are at right now. Let me tell you, Christian, the most important thing to remember when going through a storm is to continue in prayer and reading God's Word on a daily basis. How can you expect to hear Jesus call if you are not listening? When you voluntarily shut down the lines of communication between yourself and God, you aren't hurting God. You are only hurting yourself.

Contrary to what you might think, this time of my life was the most fulfilling time of personal prayer that I had ever had up to that point. Sometimes it takes some water in your boat to drive you to your knees. I was relying on God on a daily basis just to get me through each day. I was so depressed, so broken, so frustrated, that if I didn't spend time with God that day I couldn't function.

Why do we need a life-altering storm to bring us to this point of relying on God? Here's a hint: we *always* need God to sustain us. When life is going well and the sun is shining, we may *think* that we can handle everything on our own, but that's not true. We need God's mercy and grace to sustain us every day. Could it be that God is allowing this storm in your life just to remind you of that? Could it be that He just wants you to talk to Him again?

I Need to Call My Dad...

My dad is an old-school, blue collar, handy-man type of guy. He's been a mechanic since I was born and still is to this day. The man just knows how to fix things. My family growing up was on the lower end of the middle-class spectrum, so when something would break, dad would fix it. We couldn't afford to call a fancy plumber to come fix the faucet. If dad couldn't fix the problem, that meant we needed a new one! So, dad would go down to the local hardware store, purchase the most affordable new appliance or fixture, and replace the old one himself. After years of watching and helping him, he transferred that "Mr. Fixit" mentality to me. I love fixing things in my house. I enjoy spending time renovating dilapidated bathrooms, replacing broken-down appliances, and upgrading old, worn-out lights. But, whenever I run into a project that I have little or no experience in, you know the first thing I do? I call my dad. He knows what to do, and he loves spending time with me doing it.

But, what if I only called my dad when something was wrong? What if I went weeks or months at a time without ever talking to him, but then called him on the phone one day just because the furnace stopped working? I can assure you that he would still be there in a heartbeat, because he is my dad. But, do you think he would feel loved? Do you think he would feel appreciated? I guarantee you he would feel a bit taken advantage of. He would feel like I only have interest in talking to him when he can give me something, or help me out of a bad situation, or fix something that I can't fix. How would that make you feel?

I hope that you would never treat your earthly father like that, but I fear that we treat our heavenly Father this way. When things are going smoothly and our job is fine, the sun is shining and the car is running, the sky is clear and the family is healthy, our heavenly Father rarely hears from us. But, the minute a dark cloud comes into the picture and the car breaks down, or the kids get sick, or we get laid off from work, we desperately cry out to God. And how do we do it? With a sense of urgency and desperation;

maybe our voice even has a tone of frustration and anger to it. We haven't talked to our Heavenly Dad in months, but now we are angry and throwing a temper tantrum that things aren't going our way. Perhaps Dad just wants you to remember that you need Him all the time, and not just on a rainy day. Maybe, He just wants to nurture the relationship that you *say* you have with Him. Maybe, just maybe, He wants to hear your voice. When's the last time you heard His?

Through my time in God's Word and prayer, I could hear Jesus speaking to me. Not audibly, of course, but through His Word, the Holy Spirit, and the church, I could hear Him calling to me. I could hear Him crying out, "Be of good cheer! It is I! Be not afraid!" But, like the disciples, I was skeptical. I wasn't sure if I could trust Him. My faith was truly being worked out, like your pectoral muscles after a day of bench pressing, just being torn down completely until there's no strength left to even lift the bar. I could see Him, and yes, I could hear Him calling to me. I just wasn't sure what to do. The storm had rattled me to the core of my faith, and I was even second-guessing the intentions of my Heavenly Father who sent His only begotten Son into the world to die a sinner's death so that I might have everlasting life. How messed up is that? Maybe you can relate.

Let's go back to our story in Matthew 14, and see how Peter reacts to Jesus' words.

> *Matthew 14:28 And Peter answered him and said, Lord, if it be thou, bid me come unto thee on the water.*

Lord, if it be Thou...

Many a pastor and preacher have sung Peter's praises for his faith in stepping out of the boat. And don't get me wrong, he definitely did step out of the boat. We will see that in just a little bit. But, may I submit to you that Peter is actually just veiling his doubt in a cloak of feigned faith? Look at it again. After Jesus refutes the irrational responses of the disciples by confirming His identity and telling them not to fear, Peter responds with, "Lord, if it be thou…". Pause right there. Did you see it? Jesus has already showed himself to the disciples. He has walked to them supernaturally upon the sea. Just hours ago, He worked one of the greatest miracles recorded in scripture right in front of their very eyes. And Peter's response? "I'm not sure, can you prove it?"

Peter is skeptical. I'm not saying he's right, but it's understandable. I was skeptical. I lacked faith. I was doubting. I even reacted in a similar manner by saying, "Lord, if you are really there, and you really do love me, then…" Fill in the blank. Have you ever asked God, out of an exhausted and doubting heart, to prove Himself to you? I remember once in high school when I was sharing the gospel with a friend that he told me he asked God one night to prove His existence to him by bringing his dad back who had left him when he was very young. Because his dad never came back, he refused to believe in God. That doesn't sound very fair, but aren't we guilty of a similar crime when our faith is being tested amongst a tempestuous sea of swirling circumstances?

Have you ever said anything like this to God?

"God, if you're there, heal my mom from cancer."

"God, if it's you, bring my dad back."

"God, if it's you, give me my job back."

"God, if it's you, fix my marriage."

"God, if it's you, _____"

What's in your blank? Sometimes, we are so overtaken by the circumstances of our storm that we don't believe God even when He is speaking directly to us. And we want Him to prove Himself. What are you asking God to do miraculously to prove to you that He is there, that He loves you, and wants to help you? What miracle are you asking God for to confirm who He is to you? Didn't He do that when you got saved? Why does God have to prove anything to us?

Peter asks Jesus for a miracle. "Lord, if it be thou, bid me come unto thee on the water." It's really no surprise that Peter, a Jew, is asking for confirmation through a miracle here. In 1 Corinthians 1:22 it says that "Jews require a sign, and the Greeks seek after wisdom". Israel was taught in the Old Testament to look for a confirming sign from a prophet to prove that He was speaking on behalf of God. They are always looking for some kind of "dew on the fleece moment" (Judges 6:36-40) to prove that God is speaking. It's why Nicodemus said, "Rabbi, we know that thou art a teacher come from God: for no man can do these miracles that thou doest, except God be with him." (John 3:2)

So, it's no surprise that when Peter's faith is lacking he is looking for something miraculous for proof. But why is it that when we, Christians, are being tried by a storm that we also want a miracle for proof? Have we forgotten about the miracle of our salvation? Have we forgotten about all the previous victories that God has brought us through? Have we forgotten about the mountain-top spiritual high we were just on moments ago, before He told us to get on the boat? We shouldn't need Him to prove Himself to us. We should simply believe Him at His Word. After all, "for we walk by faith, not by sight." (2 Corinthians 5:7)

I think we can both agree that Jesus does not need to prove Himself to Peter. Yet, look how Jesus responds to Peter's request.

> *Matthew 14:29 And he said, Come. And when Peter was come down out of the ship, he walked on the water, to go to Jesus.*

Jesus simply replies, "Come." It may seem that Jesus is caving to Peter's lack of faith at this point, but I don't think so. I think Jesus' response is the only thing that any of us need to hear when we are toiling in rowing. Regardless of our irrational reactions and requests, Jesus has one reply to us all, "Come." He *wants* you to come to Him.

Now we can begin to appreciate Peter's faith. By the way, his faith is going to come and go multiple times in a matter of a few minutes, which is very typical of someone going through distress. But his response to Jesus' command to come is the right one: obedience and faith. Peter comes down out of the ship and walks on the water to go to Jesus.

CHAPTER 7

STEPPING OUT OF THE SHIP

Imagine this for a moment. You are in an old, rickety, wooden fishing ship in the middle of the sea. Rain is pouring down at an impossible rate. The wind is blowing so hard that everything that isn't tied down has been blown into the sea. Waves climb higher than your sails, rocking the old boat back and forth. You are holding on for dear life. You, a professional fisherman who has spent your life sailing on the sea, have never seen a storm of this magnitude. You fear for your life. The ship is falling apart. Your grip on the wheel is loosening as your strength fades. The *only* chance you have at survival is to hold on for dear life. Right?

In any storm, the safest place to be is in shelter. If you are outside when a storm hits, you seek shelter. If you are in a vehicle, you stay in the vehicle. You may pull over, but you don't get out of the car. This happened to me and my wife recently. We were driving on the highway, heading home after an appointment with her OBGYN. She was nine months pregnant at the time. As we were driving, the sky immediately became grey. It looked like a cloud was literally moving in all around us. As we gazed up at the sky in wonder, the wind picked up and rain started falling. It all happened in a matter of seconds.

It just so happened that we drove right into a microburst. If you've never heard of such a thing (I hadn't!), look it up online. It was incredible. Before I even had time to react, there were tree branches blowing across the highway and a blinding amount of rain. After about two minutes, quarter-sized hail started falling. I had to pull the car over on the side of the highway for a minute until I could see to drive again. But you know what I didn't do? I didn't get out of the car. No way. I didn't know what was going to happen, but one thing was for sure—I was staying inside the car. It was the safest place to be.

From Peter's perspective, what is the safest place to be in the storm? In the boat. I'm sure that rickety, old fishing boat didn't seem very sturdy at the time, but it was sure better than the alternative. From a human perspective, Peter's best bet for survival would be to stay in the boat and hang on for dear life. But, it turns out, when we are in a storm that Jesus is also in, the safest thing to do is also the scariest; we must step out of the boat.

WHAT IS YOUR BOAT?

When we are caught in the storm, the boat is our safety

blanket. It gives us a false sense of security that we can ride out the storm if we just hold on tight enough. Often the boat is the very thing that is holding you back from trusting Jesus. For me, it was my wallet and my savings account. I have told you that my dad was a hardworking, blue collar man, and he instilled that same work ethic in me. My dad taught me how to be a hard worker. You don't have to be smart, and you don't have to be rich to work hard. You just have to be willing. And, when you work hard, you value everything that you earned because you worked for it. It's like the 16-year-old who buys a $500 Honda Civic with the money he saved from working at Taco Bell, versus the 16-year-old who is given a brand-new 4x4 truck by his parents. Which one will take better care of their car and maintain it, and fix it, and try not to wreck it? The one who worked for it usually values it more than the other.

I was only 22 years old when I was diagnosed with Crohn's Disease. Neither my wife nor I made very much money, but both of our incomes together was enough. We lived within our means. We didn't borrow or charge money that we didn't have. Everything we had, we worked for. I didn't ask the bank for money, and I certainly never asked people for money. I worked for what we had. No handouts here! I was very prideful. But what I didn't realize was that I masked my pride with frugality and responsibility. I even had myself fooled. I was very proud of myself for taking care of my wife. I was proud that I had no debt. I was proud that I had a couple thousand dollars in my savings account. I was proud... I was... I...

That was the problem. "I". I was taking care of my wife. I was providing money. I was taking care of everything. I had previously said to the Lord, "God take it *all*", but in my heart I had said, "...but not my wallet". I didn't know that's how I felt. Honestly, I would have told you God had my heart and my wallet. I tithed over 10 percent of my income every week and gave above that to missions. I had no idea I that didn't trust God with my finances... until He took them away.

In June of that year, my bank account was almost entirely gone. Bill after bill, check after check, the money I had dwindled. I felt so helpless. My bank account was my security blanket. It was my boat. If anything went wrong, if anything broke, that would get me through it. And, in a sense, it did. Brooke and I made it through that entire year being able to pay all our medical bills with checks, not having to go into debt. But, the problem was that I relied on my savings account. God wanted me to rely on Him. He wanted me to step out of the boat and come to Him.

What is your boat? What is the safety blanket that you are clutching with a death grip, holding on for dear life? What do you refuse to let go of for fear of drowning in the sea? What have you placed a false sense of security in to get you through life, that is actually *hindering* your faith in God to provide? Are you willing to let go? Are you willing to leave it behind? Because, friend, the first step is a doozy.

Matthew 14:29 And he said, Come. And when Peter was come down out of the ship, he walked on the water, to go to Jesus.

How do you suppose Peter came down out of the ship? I don't know how big the ship was, and I don't know what it looked like, but I doubt that it had a nice staircase leading from the helm down to sea level. Maybe it had some sort of a rope ladder. Maybe it wasn't very tall. I'm not sure exactly how it happened, but in some fashion or another, Peter had to jump.

A LEAP OF FAITH

When Jesus called to Peter to "Come", Peter had to decide that he would leave the safety of the boat to jump into the roaring water below him. The very waters that were trying to capsize his boat. He had to make himself jump into the very fears and uncertainties that were upsetting the waters of his life. The first step toward Jesus isn't much of a step. It's more of a giant leap of faith, hurling yourself out of the one place your feel safe into the dark, roaring abyss that wants to consume you. It's not easy. But it is the first step you must take if you are going to go to where Jesus is. And remember, friend, Jesus is standing on the waters.

It takes faith to come to Jesus. It took faith the first time you came to Jesus—when you laid down your burdens at the cross and trusted His sacrifice to atone for your sins, to justify you, to sanctify you, and to give you eternal life. And it's going to take faith to come to Jesus in this storm. Peter may have lacked faith when He desired Jesus to prove Himself, but he seemed to waste no time in getting out of the ship to go to where Jesus was. That took faith. That took courage. That took boldness.

Can you imagine Peter's delight when he first stood up outside of the ship? I wish I could have seen that sight. After exiting the ship and jumping into the sea, Peter stands up, victoriously. The waves don't seem so big now. He's standing on water, yet his feet feel like he's standing on a rock. The wind doesn't bother him as much. The rain is more annoying now, rather than terrifying. He looks around for a moment, but then he sees Him. He sees Jesus in the distance, with arms stretched wide, waiting for him to come.

He takes a step toward Jesus. It was hard, but nowhere near as hard as getting out of the ship. His foot lands firmly on the water, with a divine surface tension providing him steady footing. He takes another step. Then another. His face lights up as he is walking on top of the very sea of fear that had him toiling in rowing for the last several hours. Everything in the world says he should be sinking into the deep, but by the power of God, he was walking! Walking forward. Walking *away* from the ship and *toward* the Lord.

His eyes were focused on Jesus as he walked: fixed on His face. With every step, he could see Jesus' face a little clearer through the wind and rain. Why had he doubted? How could he have forgotten the miracle of the bread and fish earlier that day? Surely it was smooth sailing from there. He was on the water, Jesus was on the water, and in a few minutes, He would be in His Savior's arms. All would be well.

But then, something happened. A crack of thunder, a flash of lightning. A jarring wave that landed incredibly close. He takes his eyes off Jesus for a split second and looks around. He sees the waves. He sees the rain. He's in the storm. He's no longer in the boat.

> *Matthew 14:30 But when he saw the wind boisterous, he was afraid; and beginning to sink, he cried, saying, Lord, save me.*

When Peter was walking on the water, he was looking at Jesus. His confidence was in Him. He was trusting Jesus to bring him across the waters. But, when he took his eyes off Jesus and saw the storm, he began to sink.

WHAT HAVE I GOTTEN MYSELF INTO?

If you have decided to abandon your ship to go to Jesus, you must remember to keep your eyes fixed on Him. This is not the time to be lax in your Bible reading and prayer. This is not the time to feel a false confidence in the first couple of steps you have taken. This is the time to keep focused on Christ—to keep your eyes fixed on His. If you begin to look back at the storm, you will begin to sink into the waters you were just previously walking upon.

Obviously, this is much easier said than done. Many times, once somebody has worked up the courage to jump from the safety net of their boat, they have mustered just about all the faith they can for the moment. Then, to stand up and start walking amidst the crashing waves and roaring thunder just becomes disheartening. No wonder many of us begin to sink, even after taking that first initial step of faith toward Christ. We're drained!

Spiritually, emotionally, and sometimes even physically, we're just spent. We're tired. Tired of fighting. Tired of crying. Tired of worrying. And once we've finally jumped overboard, sometimes the storm just gets to us, and we begin to wonder, like Peter, what have I gotten myself into?

Peter must've had second thoughts. The word "but" at the beginning of verse 30 in Matthew 14 contrasts Peter's intentions in verse 29 with the reality of his storm in the next verse. Peter jumped out of the ship to go to Jesus, *but*, when he saw the wind… he was afraid. Many of us have good intentions when we jump out of the ship. God has spoken to us through His Word, His Spirit, and His church, and we know what we need to do. We need to abandon our coping mechanisms and plunge into the storm, facing our fears, heading straight for Jesus. We work up enough courage to take the leap, but upon coming to our feet on the exterior of the ship, the storm looks stronger. It looks scarier. Never mind that our feet are miraculously walking on the water, we're now exposed to the elements. The rain is falling harder, and the waves are crashing closer. We begin to sink.

The reason Peter began to sink is because he took his eyes off Jesus and was distracted by the storm. Peter was focusing on the wrong thing. Rather than focusing on doing what Jesus had told him to do ("Come"), he looked around and began to size up the situation. He second-guessed his leap of faith and was now beginning to reassess the decision. He was analyzing his next move.

Why do we let things distract us from what Jesus has told us to do? Well, in a vacuum, the simple answer is our faith is weak. But practically speaking, I believe we think we need to fix our situation's individual problems, thinking that we will somehow solve the larger root problem. It's almost like getting a cold. There is no cure for the common cold, but you can medicate your symptoms with over-the-counter medicines. You can take antihistamines for mucus drainage, and nasal decongestants, and pain relievers, and so on and so forth. But, none of those medications can fix the problem. They just help alleviate the symptoms. Is it possible that we think we can alleviate the symptoms of our storm (the waves, thunder, lightning, wind) in our own power, thus ending the entire storm?

FOCUSED ON THE WAVES...

When I was going through my storm, my job wasn't helping my stress and anxiety levels. It did provide me with income and a bit of health insurance which was helping to keep the medical bills manageable. But the stress levels of working at a retail pharmacy can be very high. Maybe you've witnessed somebody at a pharmacy counter yelling at a defenseless employee because their insurance doesn't cover the medication that their doctor prescribed. The patient doesn't understand the situation, but there is really nothing that the pharmacy employee can do. They are just the middleman. This is just one small example of the many stresses that that specific occupation must deal with on a daily basis. And it was starting to get to me.

90

I was sick of my job. I was tired of the place where I worked. I was becoming very frustrated with my coworkers. I'm not saying any of these feelings are righteous, but these stressful things were magnified tenfold because of the storm I was dealing with outside of work. The burdens were piling up and weighing me down.

At this time, I had already jumped out of the boat. God had showed me this specific passage of scripture in Matthew 14 and had spoken to me through it, His Spirit, and the wonderful people in my local church edifying and encouraging me. I was putting all my faith and trust in Him to deliver me through this storm, and yet, like Peter, I was second-guessing my decision upon standing up on top of the sea. I was reassessing the situation and trying to determine what I needed to do to calm the storm in my own power; i.e., manage the magnifying factors of my stress and anxiety.

So, I started looking for another job. I put out resumes. I applied at every pharmacy and hospital within a 30-minute drive of where I lived. I didn't care where I worked, but I figured that anywhere had to be better than where I was. I prayed hard that God would give me a different job, completely convinced that it was the largest source of pain in my life. It wasn't, but I was convinced. I was afraid, and I was sinking. I was distracted from Jesus. I was focused on the waves.

Eventually, I did get a call from another pharmacy. It was a 20-mile drive from my house, while my current job was only about two miles away. It also was a pay decrease. But I didn't care. I would drive farther, and I would take less money just to get away.

Surely the grass was greener over there. Surely the sea was calmer. Remember how the disciples had some pretty irrational thoughts during their storm? I can relate. I was thinking incredibly irrationally at this point. But I was convinced that this was the right move to make.

The crazy thing is, I was so relieved to get another job offer that I convinced myself it was an answer to prayer! Yes, I had been praying for God to give me another job, but I didn't really pray and ask Him if this was the right one. I was so anxious to try and calm the storm myself that I figured this opportunity had to be "of the Lord". We talk ourselves into this a lot, don't we, Christian? Just because a seemingly good opportunity presents itself, we assume that it is God answering our prayer; but, more often than not, it is simply our desire that we haven't actually prayed to God about. If I would have been patient, kept my eyes on Christ, and pursued Him for an answer, I have no doubt He would have told me to wait on Him.

But I didn't wait on Him. I took the job. I put in my two-week notice and left my old employer and coworkers in a not-so-respectable hurry. I had convinced myself that different would be better, but I didn't know that. I was distracted by the storm and had stopped looking to Jesus for power to walk on the water. I was flailing about in my own power, trying to stay afloat.

I started the new job at a much smaller, privately-owned pharmacy. It wasn't the large retail pharmacy in the center of a super-market that I was used to. It seemed calmer. It had less foot traffic. It appeared to be less stressful. I had only two coworkers in the pharmacy. Surely, this job would be a laid-back, worry-free environment that was worth the drive and the pay decrease. What could go wrong?

Well, as it turns out, when you are stuck in a storm of life and are thinking irrationally, you don't have the best discernment. You don't think about the question, "Why is this small, quaint, seemingly-perfect job looking for a new employee? What happened to the last one?" I'll spare you the details and just say that after the first week, the stress levels went through the roof. I hadn't thought about how long it would take for me to get used to the new workplace environment, as well as the new software used for checking and billing prescriptions. I also didn't realize that the less employees you have, the more work each of you have to do when the store is busy. I hadn't visited the store when it was busy. I assumed it was always slow. That was a bad assumption. The temporary relief was quickly subsiding, and I felt the waters rising. My knees were wet. I was sinking. What had I gotten myself into?

SINKING

Let's look back at what Peter did when he began to sink:

> *Matthew 14:30 But when he saw the wind boisterous, he was afraid; and beginning to sink, he cried, saying, Lord, save me.*

As Peter began to plunge rapidly into the waters he was just previously walking on, his reaction was the only thing he could think of to do at the time. He cried out, "Lord, save me." After doubt, worry, fear, disbelief, irrational reactions, and distractions, Peter finally gave up trying to conquer this storm on his own and cried out to Jesus to save him—like a public pool-goer thrashing about in the deep end, crying out to the lifeguard between gulps of air and pool water.

"I'm drowning! I can't save myself! If you don't intervene, I'll surely drown!"

Have you been here? Maybe that's where you're at right now? Maybe that's why you picked up this book—as some last-ditch attempt to find some sort of life-preserver to cling to. That's where I was after I switched jobs to a new employer. I had no moves left, and no new ideas. I was drowning, and I knew that I had no other options. As I was thrashing in the rapidly rising waters, I cried out in anguish, "Lord, save me! I'm in over my head! The last year was the greatest 12 months of my life, but now in these last six months, I'm completely devasted! I have nothing left, and I'm completely powerless. Please, God, intervene!"

And He did.

Matthew 14:31 And immediately Jesus stretched forth his hand, and caught him, and said unto him, O thou of little faith, wherefore didst thou doubt?

When Peter cried out to Jesus to save him, Jesus acted immediately. Without hesitation, He stretched forth his hand and caught him. How far away was Jesus when Peter began to sink? How many steps had Peter made toward Jesus before he began to sink? The Bible doesn't say. What we do know is that Jesus was there immediately. It didn't matter where Peter was in relation to Him, He was there immediately to catch him.

The God of the universe was there with outstretched hand to pull him out of the sea. This storm was life-altering for Peter, but for God, this was nothing. This is the God who spoke the universe into existence. This is the God of Peter's fathers who witnessed Him deliver them from Egypt, part the Red Sea, provide manna in the wilderness, bring them across Jordan, and defeat their enemies. This same God, who can control the wind and waves with His words, was there to save Peter in the midst of his storm. Compared to God, this storm was of such inconsequential size that it probably resembled the significance of an atom to you or me. But the greatness of the storm did not matter to Jesus; for when a follower of Jesus Christ calls out to Him, He is there to respond. He always has been, and He always will be.

WHY DID YOU DOUBT?

Notice what Jesus says to Peter after He catches him, "O thou of little faith, wherefore didst thou doubt?" Jesus is simply asking Peter what we are all wondering to ourselves. Why didn't you trust Jesus? What happened to your faith, Peter? Surely, if I could physically see Jesus standing in front of *me*, then I wouldn't have any problem trusting Him. Well, perhaps we think more highly of ourselves than we ought. For we have the divinely inspired and perfectly preserved words of the Almighty God collecting dust on our end table as we flail about in the waves. Maybe we should ask ourselves the same question: O thou of little faith, why do you doubt?

The simple answer to that question is that we have taken our eyes off Jesus. Doubt, defined by scripture as a lack of faith (Romans 14:23), happens when our focus on Christ is distracted by our surrounding circumstances. When we allow our vision to be clouded by the storm around us, we lose sight of Jesus and the promises He gives us in His Word. You cannot look at Jesus *and* the storm. You must make a conscious decision to keep your eyes on Jesus rather than the storm, because your natural tendency is to focus on the potential danger around you. But don't do it, Christian. You must trust the Word of God in front of you more than your natural inclination to doubt your own power to survive the inclement weather. Of course, you can't survive this on your own. But you aren't supposed to. You are supposed to trust Him.

After only six weeks of working at this new pharmacy, one of the pastors at my church called and told me that they had an opening for a full-time maintenance man. It wasn't a ministry position, but I didn't care. I had the opportunity to work at my very own church—cleaning it, maintaining it, and taking care of it. I didn't care at all that I was going to be scrubbing toilets and vacuuming hallways. Jesus was pulling me out of the sea.

On a Monday morning, I went to my employer and apologetically told them that I would be leaving them in two weeks. They were understandably frustrated; they had just hired me six weeks prior. But they understood that I couldn't pass up this opportunity to work for my church. But, what was about to happen in the next couple of days, neither myself nor my boss would have ever seen coming.

Just three days later, on Thursday morning, everyone walked into work just like any other day. The pharmacist unlocked the building. The few employees, including myself, walked in and began our normal morning routine. Several hours passed and everything was business as usual. But, everyone began to wonder, who are the men in suits who just walked in the building?

Everyone watched the men talk in a hushed tone to the manager of the retail store. They looked over and nodded to the pharmacist in a manner that implied, "We need you too". Before he went to meet with them and the store manager in a private office, he mentioned to me, "That's corporate. This can't be good."

Not very long after, all the employees of the small store had been called into the office. Confusion and tension were building in the silence of the cramped room. A man in a suit began to speak to us—slowly, apologetically, but matter-of-factly. He informed us that our store had just been bought out by the pharmacy down the street. Further, today would be our last day open. When we closed the doors that night, our store was closed for good.

None of us could believe it. Obviously, stores get bought out all the time by other companies. But I had never heard of a store getting bought out and closing within one day. At the very least, I would have thought the retail manager and the pharmacist would have been told prior. But I could tell by their reactions that they had no clue. This was news to all of us. At 7:00 pm, we would all be unemployed.

Then, all of a sudden, it struck me—I'm not unemployed. I'm only a few days into my two-week notice. I had another job lined up at the church, and I could simply start a bit earlier! Coincidence? Definitely not. Luckily for me, God's mercy was providing for me despite my poor decisions. God knew from the time I took that job that the pharmacy was going to close in six weeks. Had I sought Him, and kept my eyes on Him, perhaps I would have heard Him telling me to be patient and stay put. But, thankfully, God is good and His mercy endureth forever!

Psalm 118:1 O give thanks unto the LORD; for he is good: because his mercy endureth for ever.

We were instructed to call each of our customers that had prescriptions ready to be picked up and ask them if they could come in that day. We had to let each one of them know that we had been bought by the competing pharmacy, that we were closing for good that night, and, if they couldn't make it in to pick up their prescription, that they could pick it up the next day at the other location. This was stressful work. The other employees were frazzled to say the least. We had a lot of work to accomplish, and there wasn't much incentive to work hard or with a good attitude.

But for me, I was just thankful for God's provision. I was also thankful that I got to start my job at the church sooner. So, I worked as hard as I could and tried to keep a smile on my face for the confused customers. I tried to navigate around the understandable disgruntled mood of my coworkers. This actually caught the attention of the corporate men in suits who were helping us get things done, and the CEO of the small chain of retail pharmacies actually gave me his card and told me to contact him if I needed a job in the future! What an encouragement that was, to see that I could be a witness for Christ by simply working hard with a smile. Those men knew that I was going to work for my church. They knew I was a Christian and wanted to be a pastor someday. I hope that I planted a small seed in their lives about how Christians react in difficult times, because certainly this was the first time in a while that I felt like things were looking up. I had started to sink, but as I cried out to Jesus with one final plea of desperation, He caught me. I didn't deserve it, but He caught me—immediately.

> *Matthew 14:32 And when they were come into the ship, the wind ceased.*

THE WIND CEASED...

Scripture doesn't tell us if Peter responded to Jesus' question, "O thou of little faith, wherefore didst thou doubt?" That doesn't mean that he didn't respond; all it means is that his response wasn't important. The significance is Christ's question, not Peter's response. The question needed to resonate through Peter so that he understood that there wasn't any reason to doubt in the first place. He needed to understand that Jesus was always there with him, walking on the waves, ready to help.

Do you feel Jesus asking you that question today, Christian? Why have you doubted? Why have you allowed yourself to sink this far into the Slough of Despond, like John Bunyan's character Christian in *The Pilgrim's Progress*? Your response isn't that important... as long as you understand where you have erred. If you've come through the storm learning the lesson God desired for you to learn, the only response to Christ's question you need to have is to embrace Him and say, "Abba, Father".

After Jesus pulls Peter out of the sea, He takes him back into the ship. And, low and behold, the wind ceased. The force of nature that immobilized the disciples was stopped, immediately. The wind didn't slow down until it stopped at Jesus' command. The entire scene was so extraordinary that the crew of the ship understood just who this Man coming into the ship was—and I don't mean Peter! This other guy, the One that they initially thought was a ghost, had to be the Son of God.

> *Matthew 14:33 Then they that were in the ship came and worshipped him, saying, Of a truth thou art the Son of God.*

When I left the pharmacy the night it closed, I had mixed emotions. I was grateful that God had provided this job at the church so that I wouldn't be unemployed. I was thankful that He extended mercy to me, even though I followed my own desires to take this job at the new pharmacy in the first place. I was happy that I got to start working at the church sooner than I had planned. But, as I thought about it longer, I was just in awe of who God was.

He was the lone constant in my life during this trial, and He revealed that to me. He manifested His power over circumstances in my life by making the wind cease. He showed me His love by reaching down to me and pulling me out of the sea. He proved His promise to finish the work He had begun in me until He returns one day (Philippians 1:6). And, possibly for the first time in my Christian life, I personally *experienced* God's provision, upholding, and sustaining. On my 20-mile drive home that night, all I could manage to say was, "Of a truth, thou art the Son of God." I worshipped Him through tear-filled eyes all the way home.

CHAPTER 8

ARRIVING IN GENNESARET

Matthew 14:34 And when they were gone over, they came into the land of Gennesaret.

I suppose this verse is the reason for writing this book. This verse brought much hope to me during my trial because it showed the light at the end of the tunnel. The conclusion of this story in Matthew chapter 14 is, simply put, when they had gone through all of this, they arrived at the destination Christ had given them.

God spends 13 verses recording this story for us in the Bible. 12 of them are focused on the storm, the unfolding events around it, and the disciples. Just one verse recounts their arrival to Gennesaret. The journey was more significant for the disciples than the destination. The lessons learned on the sea of tribulation were more important than arriving where Jesus had told them to go.

Let this verse be an encouragement to you, Christian. If you are caught in the middle of the storm, let this scripture resound in your heart. When they were gone over, they came into the land of Gennesaret. In other words, after they had gone through all of that—all of the trial, all of the fear, all of the anguish—they reached their destination. After going through the storm and experiencing Jesus' provision, they arrived where He had told them to go. In fact, they arrived exactly *where* Jesus wanted them to be, exactly *when* He wanted them to get there.

NO TURNING BACK...

Don't spend your life toiling in rowing. Don't spend your life stuck in a storm, angry at God for the waves. I fear that many Christians spend their life here, or worse—they give up entirely and just give up on God. Maybe they turn to a bottle to solve their problems, or maybe a pill, or sex, or their job. Maybe they don't do something that drastic, but maybe they just lose their passion. Perhaps some Christians don't make it through the storm and just assume that God didn't mean what He told them. Or, maybe they misheard. Or, perhaps God had just let them down. Many well-intentioned Christians turn back when the going gets tough, because they forgot that their journey is not a vacation, but one of spiritual warfare and growth.

This is all-too common in Christianity. In *The Pilgrim's Progress*, the main character, Christian, comes upon two men who have abandoned their journeys because it became too difficult:

> Now when Christian arrived at the top of the Hill, two men came running toward him in full flight from the opposite direction. The name of one was Timorous, and the name of the other Mistrust. To these Christian enquired, "Sirs, what is the matter since you are both running the wrong way?" Hence Timorous replied "We were making our pilgrimage toward the City of Zion and had reached beyond this Hill Difficulty; but then the further we went the more danger we encountered. As a result we decided to turn about and return home; so we are now fast on our way."[2]

When Israel exited Egypt, under the power of God and the leading of Moses and Aaron, the people were excited—*initially*. But the storm started quickly as their backs were against the Red Sea, and Pharaoh and his army of chariots pursued them. Very quickly, many of them were mad at Moses for bringing them out of Egypt.

> *Exodus 14:11-12*
> *11 And they said unto Moses, Because there were no graves in Egypt, hast thou taken us away to die in the wilderness? wherefore hast thou dealt thus with us, to carry us forth out of Egypt?*
> *12 Is not this the word that we did tell thee in Egypt, saying, Let us alone, that we may serve the Egyptians? For it had been better for us to serve the Egyptians, than that we should die in the wilderness.*

---

[2] John Bunyan, *The Pilgrim's Progress*, rev. Barry Horner (New York: Reformation Press, 1999), 55, http://bunyanministries.org/books/pp_full_text.pdf

How irrational! How could they be mad at being delivered from bondage? How could they desire to be back in Egypt, a place where they had been enslaved for 400 years and forced to do hard labor? In fact, several times in the wanderings of Israel in the wilderness, the people murmur against Moses, and ultimately against God, for bringing them out of Egypt—and they try to go back!

Did you know that the nation of Israel in the Old Testament is a picture of the New Testament Christian? That means that the nation of Israel, as a whole, is a picture of *you*, Christian. God delivering Israel (His son, Exodus 4:22) from the bondage of Egypt (a picture of sin and the world) is a picture of God delivering you from the bondage of sin and the world when you got saved. If you can understand this simple truth, reading the Old Testament will become much more interesting! The trials and tribulations of the nation of Israel as they travel through the wilderness picture for us the trials and tribulations of the Christian as he or she grows in Christ. There are many lessons God gives us through Israel as an example (1Corinthians 10:1-10).

Understanding this picture, is it really a surprise that Israel wanted to turn back when circumstances became hard? It is easy for us to judge them with the advantage of hindsight, but I know that I would have done the same thing, because I did when I was going through my storm. Thankfully, God is a loving Father who desires to see us grow through these tribulations, and to trust and rely in Him more.

My arrival at Gennesaret seemed, at the time, to be very quick.

I assumed that my Gennesaret was to just trust God more and work at the church. But that was the analysis of young Christian. With the advantage of experience and hindsight, I can look back on what God taught me through the storm that has prepared me for where I am today.

THE END?

I started working as a maintenance man at our church in the fall of that year. I was also asked to lead our Middle School student ministry that year. Looking back, I know that it was no coincidence that God waited to give me that ministry responsibility until after He had proved me through the storm. That was part of the destination. That was part of Gennesaret for me.

But it didn't end there. I continued to grow in my faith and seek God. I still wanted to be all-in and do whatever He wanted me to do, whenever and wherever He called me to do it. Two years later, my church hired me onto the pastoral staff full time to be the Youth Pastor. It was my dream—to be the youth pastor at the church where I had grown up, over my former youth group. I couldn't believe it! This is what God had in store for me. Truly, I was living in the dream and vision God had revealed to me several years ago.

I started writing this book in 2014. It's alright, you can laugh. I'm slow when it comes to creative things. Any song or poem that I've written typically begins as a chorus that comes to me in the shower. I write it down in a journal, and it sits there for years until a verse comes to me. I've written songs that took me five years to complete. That's just how my mind works—slowly.

But God knows that, so He works with me slowly. I previously thought that I was just procrastinating in finishing this book. What I didn't realize was that God wasn't done telling me the story. I couldn't have possibly finished this book any earlier, because the ending is just now coming to true fulfillment. I'm just now seeing my true Gennesaret on the horizon.

After four years of serving as the Youth Pastor of my church and six years in youth ministry total, my wife and I are raising funds to be missionaries to the country of Hungary. My father's family is Hungarian; in fact, my last name is a common Hungarian name. This small tidbit got me introduced to a pastor in Lambertville, Michigan whose church had been providing evangelical summer camps for Hungarian orphans. I went on my first trip to Hungary in 2014 and have been going back ever since.

10 years of summer camp ministries in Hungary have yielded hundreds of young Christian converts of all ages. After years of serving in Hungary, praying, and consulting God's Word, God has confirmed that He is calling me and my wife to move to Hungary and plant churches. The fruit is unavoidable. There are sheep without a shepherd in Hungary, waiting for someone to come and disciple them. What I didn't know in 2013 was that this is where God wanted me to ultimately go. What God had been preparing me for is to change my address for the gospel and take God's Good News to a people group that is only three percent evangelical.

What I didn't know in 2013 was that God was responding to my claim that I was willing do whatever He wanted me to do and go wherever He wanted me to go. The storm that followed was a litmus test—a filter to see if I truly meant what I said. God was preparing a work in another country, but He needed to prove me to see if I would be willing to allow Him to grow me into the man that He needed me to be for this task.

Little did I know that the Lambertville church who started this ministry 10 years ago had been praying since the beginning for God to send a missionary to Hungary to continue to plow the soil they had been sowing. How humbling to realize that I am a small part of God answering their prayers! But, in contrast, if I had decided to not trust God and to not follow the burden He had placed in my heart, I would have missed out on what God is doing through that church on the other side of the world. How joyful and adventurous our lives can be if we will simply trust God and do anything He asks of us!

FINAL THOUGHTS...

Getting on the boat is easy. Obeying Jesus' command when the weather is nice isn't incredibly difficult. It's navigating the storms that come after the journey begins that's hard. Many never make it to the destination because the waters swallow them up in unbelief. But for those who rely on Christ, keep their eyes fixed on Him, and patiently follow Him across the sea, the valuable lessons learned in the journey make the destination that much more monumental. The lessons learned on the sea of sanctification make us the men and women God wants us to be—and the tools He can use for His purposes. There is no greater joy than coming out of the refiner's fire looking more like Christ and becoming more useful for His work.

But there is another secondary function of the storms we go through. Yes, the most important function is growing our faith and making us more like Christ. But there is yet another purpose for the storms that we would be remiss to ignore. Remember in Joshua 4, when God told Joshua to set up the pile of 12 stones when they crossed the Jordan river into the Promised Land? That pile of stones had two purposes: 1) it was a memorial for the children of Israel to remember what God had brought them through, and 2) it was to serve as a lesson to teach their children (who didn't have this experience) about God, His goodness, His might, and His provision.

We must not devalue the importance of the experiences God allows us to go through in our lives in order to share that story of God's power with others. That is the reason I've written this book. I simply wish to share with as many people as possible how God worked in my life, so that my experience can be encouraging and uplifting to others. Not only is our testimony of God's grace in our lives powerful to the lost world, but it exhorts our fellow brothers and sisters in Christ. It is cause for joy, celebration, and praise!

It could also be what someone needs to hear who is going through a similar experience. Hasn't it been uplifting to read these words of a fellow Christian who went through something similar to what you're going through? Of course, the circumstances are different, but the testimony of a fellow Christian's past experiences in the storms and pitfalls of life are an encouragement to those who are currently experiencing a trial of their faith. Don't lose sight of that. God can use your story to impact the lives of people around you!

> *Galatians 6:2 Bear ye one another's burdens, and so fulfil the law of Christ.*

We have people in our church who have checkered pasts—people who God brought out of major sin, addiction, and other hardships—who use their experiences of failure and success to minister to people with similar situations. It's how God designed it. That is what the church is for.

> *2 Corinthians 1:4 Who comforteth us in all our tribulation, that we may be able to comfort them which are in any trouble, by the comfort wherewith we ourselves are comforted of God.*

So, whatever situation God is bringing you through now, He desires you to use that story as a lesson for teaching others about how powerful He is. He wants you to encourage and exhort others with your experiences of His love and grace, along with the scriptures that guided you through those storms. Use what God has taught you to help others navigate the storms in their lives— that's what discipleship is all about! Teaching others to walk with Christ and reproduce sons and daughters of God.

> *2 Timothy 2:2 And the things that thou hast heard of me among many witnesses, the same commit thou to faithful men, who shall be able to teach others also.*

If anything, maybe this perspective can help strengthen your faith in God enough to keep going through the storm. Understanding why storms happen, and how God wants to use them in and through us, can help us endure them. Remember, wherever you are, Christian, Christ is in the storm with you. He will never leave you or forsake you. The Holy Spirit took up residence inside of you at the moment of your salvation, and no matter where you go, He is there.

> *Psalm 139:7-10*
> *7 Whither shall I go from thy spirit? or whither shall I flee from thy presence?*
> *8 If I ascend up into heaven, thou art there: if I make my bed in hell, behold, thou art there.*
> *9 If I take the wings of the morning, and dwell in the uttermost parts of the sea;*
> *10 Even there shall thy hand lead me, and thy right hand shall hold me.*

We may not have the physical body of Jesus walking toward us, calling out to us with His physical vocal cords. But we do have a "more sure word of prophecy" (2 Peter 1:19). We have the Word of God. We have the infallible words of Creator God who promised that, till heaven and earth pass away, not one jot or one tittle will pass from the law (Matthew 5:18). We have the mind of

Christ (1 Corinthians 2:16) recorded for us in a Book that at any moment we can pick up and read and commune with God the Father. So, Christian, you have no excuse to not seek God in your storm. For we are promised that if we will seek Him and draw nigh to Him, He will draw nigh to us.

> *James 4:8 Draw nigh to God, and he will draw nigh to you. Cleanse your hands, ye sinners; and purify your hearts, ye double minded.*
>
> *Psalm 145:18 The LORD is nigh unto all them that call upon him, to all that call upon him in truth.*

Go to Him, Christian. Jump out of the boat and run to Him. He is in the storm, and He is calling to you. He desires to bring you through this storm to grow your faith and to use you in the lives of many others. Will you trust Him? Will you allow Him to build a pile of stones that serves as a memorial of His power, provision, and faithfulness for the rest of your life? Will you remember the promises that He records for you in scripture that describe His thoughts and desires for you, even though the waves around you seem to say the contrary?

> *Psalm 139:17-18*
> *17 How precious also are thy thoughts unto me, O God! how great is the sum of them!*
> *18 If I should count them, they are more in number than the sand: when I awake, I am still with thee.*
>
> *Jeremiah 29:11 For I know the thoughts that I think toward you, saith the LORD, thoughts of peace, and not of evil, to give you an expected end.*

If you will, that doesn't mean it will be easy. I'm not saying that your journey will be smooth sailing from here on out. But I can guarantee you, on the authority of the Scripture, that your life will matter and God will use you. God doesn't call the qualified, he qualifies the called. If you will let Him qualify you, He will use you.

> *1Thessalonians 5:24 Faithful is he that calleth you, who also will do it.*

It's entirely up to you, Christian. Gennesaret is just beyond the horizon, just beyond the borders of your faith. Will you quit? Or will you allow the One who calms the seas with the sound of His voice to calm your soul and to bring you to the destination He has for you?

That is the journey to Gennesaret.

ABOUT THE AUTHOR

Kale Horvath is a Missionary to the country of Hungary. He served four years on staff as the Youth Pastor at First Baptist Church of New Philadelphia, Ohio, the church where he grew up, was discipled, and trained. Kale graduated from Living Faith Bible Institute in 2017 and was ordained into the gospel ministry that same year. He and his wife, Brooke, were married in 2012. They have one son, Judah, who was born in 2018.